To Walk in the Kingdom

To Walk in the Kingdom

MARVA SEDORE

CHRISTIAN HERALD BOOKS
Chappaqua, New York

We acknowledge with appreciation permission to quote from:
HOLY BIBLE: New International Version. Copyright © 1978 by the New York International Bible Society. Used by permission of Zondervan Bible Publishers.

Library of Congress Cataloging in Publication Data

Sedore, Marva J.
To walk in the kingdom.

1. Bible. N.T. Luke XII—Meditations.
2. Christian life—Biblical teaching. I. Title.
BS2595.4.S43 226'.4077 81-68638
ISBN 0-86693-003-5 AACR2

MEMBER OF
EVANGELICAL CHRISTIAN
PUBLISHERS ASSOCIATION

First Edition
CHRISTIAN HERALD BOOKS, 40 Overlook Drive, Chappaqua,
New York 10514
Printed in the United States of America

To the board of Christians
Equipped for Ministry
and to the participants
in the EPHESUS Community,
with gratitude
for all that you have taught me
about the Kingdom of God

Contents

Introduction 9

1. Not Hypocrisy, but Commitment 12
2. To Be the Friend of Jesus 24
3. To Fear and Love God 36
4. The Use of Our Tongues 45
5. Not Grasping for Authority and Avoiding Covetousness 59
6. Hearing a Parable About Priorities 71
7. Seven Reasons Not to Worry 82
8. The Gift of the Kingdom 99
9. To Care for the Poor 110
10. The Correlation of Treasure and Heart 123
11. The Delight of Christ's Surprises 133
12. The Blessedness of Being Prepared 145
13. To Be Faithful and Wise Stewards 157
14. Reading the Signs of the Times 170

Appendix A: Resources on Helping the Poor 184

Appendix B: Resources for Studying Luke 186

Introduction

I feel I am ready to write this book. The verses of Luke 12 seem to summarize the major movements of my Christian growth and life right now. However, I know, too, that if I were to write this book next year it would come out very much different, for the same verses of the Scriptures will be cutting me in new ways by then. If we are faithful in studying the Scriptures, we will be constantly growing as Christians. God has given us His Word in order that we might always be learning new things about Him, about ourselves, and about what our relationship with Him involves.

Luke 12 is a critically important chapter to me because it contains many of the most important principles for the stewardship of our Christian lives. Its verses tell us how to be good stewards of our minds and bodies and souls and spirits. Today these lessons are especially meaningful to me because I have just recently attended a life-changing retreat, led by members of Wellspring, part of the Church of the Saviour in Washington, D.C. I returned from that retreat with a deeper Joy in the meaning of my life and the privilege of serving Jesus as part of His Kingdom.

These lessons are also meaningful because a dear friend, for whom I have been concerned for a long time, made some wrong choices recently. He has taken a course of action contrary to God's principles and, therefore, ultimately destructive to his life. That is heartbreaking.

Out of the pain I am motivated to teach. I believe wholeheartedly that if people learn to study the Scriptures, they will learn to delight in who God is and in what His plan for a life of abundance and fulfillment and Joy involves. Nevertheless, at various times all of us settle for less than the best because we choose our own desires rather than His. It is absolutely essential, on the contrary, to meditate upon His Word daily, to let His revelation be constantly the guiding force of our lives. His Word will transform us.

The twelfth chapter of Luke is a stupendously transforming bit of God's Word. In just a few verses we are challenged to take seriously what it means to be the people of God, to be participants in His Kingdom and eager to extend that Kingdom to others. If we could learn the basic principles of this chapter, we would find ourselves more effective in serving the Kingdom; we would enjoy more our position in that Kingdom; and we would be more able to speak about that Kingdom to those still searching for it.

Two dangerous extremes make it vitally important for us to have a clearly defined Kingdom theology. One danger is to think that as the people of God, we are "the King's Kids," called to lives of ease, comfort, and luxury. That heresy leads to possessiveness, exclusivism, and a gluttony that destroys the credibility of our witness.

On the other hand, it is wrong to think that to be a Christian means to suffer deprivation, to walk around with a gloomy face, not to participate in anything that is fun. That heresy leads to legalism, a different kind of exclusivism, and a lack of Joy that also destroys the credibility of our witness.

To participate in the Kingdom means to walk in the middle, seeking a balance between overindulgence and asceticism in every area of our lives. I think that the balance is difficult for each of us to find, but I believe that the Scriptures are written to enable us to find and enjoy it.

So I invite you to come with me into the life-transforming verses of Luke 12. I could hardly begin to know everything there is to know about those verses. But I am asking them seriously to challenge my life intensely. I cannot be the same after I have thoroughly meditated upon them. I pray that as you read these expositional and devotional comments you will learn not only new insights into the truths they contain, but also new skills for further, deeper study of the Scriptures on your own.

Our God is eternally worth knowing. Let us begin to know Him better in a consistent pursuit of His Word. It is, indeed, His good pleasure to give us the Kingdom.

Marva J. Sedore
EPIPHANY 1981

1 Not Hypocrisy, but Commitment

"Meanwhile, when a crowd of many thousands had gathered, so that they were trampling on one another, Jesus began to speak first to his disciples, saying: 'Be on your guard against the yeast of the Pharisees, which is hypocrisy. There is nothing concealed that will not be disclosed, or hidden that will not be made known. What you have said in the dark will be heard in the daylight, and what you have whispered in the ear in the inner rooms will be proclaimed from the housetops.' "

—Luke 12:1-3

It was a joy to give the wedding sermon for David and Cindy. I had been extremely nervous about it because I knew that most of the people observing the ceremony didn't really care about the Christian dimensions of the service. But how I spoke that message was radically transformed when I suddenly realized that I didn't have to speak to anyone else in the church.

It was David and Cindy who wanted to hear my words about commitment to God and to each other and about the strength available to God's people for the working out of their marriages. What an experience it was to watch their faces as I spoke! Their eyes were fixed on me with fervent intensity in an eager desire to hear every little word. What I said was meant for them, but I was glad that the rest of the crowd overheard. I wanted them also to know the responsibilities of Christian marriage. And they should at least hear what discipleship means in case they might want to try it out.

The situation was very much the same when Jesus began preaching the messages of Luke 12. The crowds were so large that they are described with a word best translated "myriads." The term denotes literally tens of thousands, but is often used in the Scriptures to mean a very large crowd. The use of the definite article in the original Greek seems to imply that it was the customary crowd. Many people usually gathered around Jesus. His authority and the news about His miracles attracted many onlookers.

In the scene that is set before us, however, Jesus is almost oblivious to those crowds. He has important lessons for the disciples to learn. In his Greek construction Luke stresses the word *first*. These instructions were meant primarily for the chosen few. They were available to all, but not everyone would want to hear them.

That is the case with this book. The message is primarily for disciples. I'd like for the whole world to hear its call, but not many will like it. There is going to be a lot of tough stuff in this book. The words of Jesus in the twelfth chapter of Luke call His followers to some difficult decisions, to some times of struggle, to some questions of priorities and values that are not easy. What will you do with them?

Just today I had to wrestle again with the question of my own commitment. Last week I went to an ecstatic, life-changing retreat. I came back thoroughly refreshed and confidently sure of my calling. Those feelings were richly confirmed as I spent the next two days discussing the Joys of the retreat with a very dear friend. And finally today I had a day of vacation in Seattle with two other members of the Christian community in which I live.

But while in Seattle we went to visit some friends and learned the painful news that a former counselee of mine has moved into a sinful sexual relationship. I felt like I'd been hit with a sledgehammer, and, doubled over with grief, I asked God, "Why couldn't you have let the Joy last for more than a week?"

I felt overwhelmed by the pain and sickness and ugliness of the world gone amuck. Finally I'd had a week that had lifted me above the responsibility and challenge that I constantly face in my work, and now my cloud nine had evaporated, and I had plummeted and shattered on the rocks of reality. *Why is ministry so hard?* I demanded to know.

That is the problem often in my own discipleship. I want the good times to last forever. I long for eternity in everything. And when the happiness is shoved aside by grim reality, I want to back out of my commitment to be Christ's person in this broken world. I want to hide away in my own little paradise and ignore the suffering of others. *I've been through enough suffering myself,* I think. *I deserve a bit of rest and comfort.*

I want to have it as easy as the rest of the crowd. The setting of the scene at the beginning of Luke 12 hits home with me. Jesus goes on giving His instructions to the committed ones, and I try to get lost in the myriads.

There are lots of people—including you and me at times—trying to run away like that. Luke says the crowds were so great that they were trampling on one another. That is not such an easy existence either, if we look honestly at the choices. To be lost in the shuffle makes me a nonentity. On the other hand, to choose to be a disciple demands my death.

Last week it was easy to make that choice. I was ecstatic. I loved my work. I knew my uniqueness. I felt chosen and called and loved by God. People who surrounded me were committed to Him also, and we rejoiced together in the privilege of our calls.

But this week I am back in the pain. Now it is not so easy to be a disciple, one who follows in the steps of Jesus. As Peter tells us in his first letter, the example that Jesus left for us to follow was one of suffering (1 Pet. 2:21). Luke stresses the same thing by using the scene of Jesus' setting His face to go to Jerusalem as a turning point for the whole gospel account (see Luke 9:51 and its context). Jesus set His face to go to Jerusalem; nothing could stop Him from pursuing His goal. And His only reason for going there was to die.

Do we want to choose to set our faces also? Do we want to say with Thomas, "Let us also go, that we may die with him" (John 11:16)?

Fortunately, that is not the end of the invitation. If it were, I would not write this book. Why should I want to invite you to a life of misery and pain? But Luke gives us an important key. He tells us that Jesus set His face to go to Jerusalem when the time was drawing near for His being taken up to heaven. The ascension is the critical event for Luke. At that point, Jesus assumed the lordship that He had voluntarily laid aside to accomplish His work of salvation for us. As the gospel of John points out, the gift of the Holy Spirit was made possible by the ascension (John 16:7), as were Christ's constant intercession and presence with us. When it was time for His glory to be manifested, Jesus set His face to die. For the Joy set before Him, the writer to the Hebrews says, He endured the cross and despised the shame (Hebrews 12:2). There was more to His choice than the agony of the cross.

We are also called to glory. Paul reckons that the sufferings of this present time aren't worth comparing to the glory that is to be revealed in us (Rom. 8:18). It is important for us to understand that glory not only in a far-off, heavenly sense. In addition, that glory is revealed in us now—even, sometimes, at the most terrible moments of struggle.

It will be worth it if you decide to pay attention to the lessons that Jesus gives in Luke 12. If you listen carefully to His instructions about stewardship, you will find yourself freed from the bonds of materialism, the hypertensions of hypocrisy, the worries about words. All the lessons of this chapter will have these double sides—the struggles that everyone shares and the Joy that is added for the believers because we alone can know for sure that all the struggles will be worth it.

That realization hit me today as I was meditating during my swimming workout. The grief of last night made swimming hard for the first 61 laps. Suddenly, however, on the 62nd lap, everything broke free. My lungs and muscles finally were working effectively, and it was easy to swim the rest of a mile and a quarter. In fact, the 82nd lap was completed without my noticing, because it was so grace-full.

A bit of theologizing brought clearly the recognition that my Christian life is like that. There are the struggles, but there is also the ease, the Joy, the grace. The water had supported me throughout the whole grim time of workout. I just hadn't realized its faithfulness until my body could cooperate and receive its support.

The same truth applies to discipleship. God is faithful. No matter what is going on in the texture of our lives, His love for us is always the same. I love the picture of faithfulness in Pachelbel's *Canon in D,* in which the string bass plays the same series of eight notes throughout the entire piece. No matter what the intricate developments taking place in the constantly changing texture, the *cantus firmus* remains constant and pictures for me God's immutability. God *is* faithful!

It is His faithfulness that invites us to discipleship. We can know that He will be true to His promises, and this chapter of Luke is loaded with them. In fact, we will notice as we work through its lessons that Jesus alternates between sections of amazing good news and those that call us to rugged commitment. The good news always is the undergirding that makes our response possible.

We are not disciples because Christ forces us to be. David and Cindy listened to their wedding sermon because they wanted to. They knew that the rewards of working at their marriage with Christ at the center would be vastly worth it. (And their experience several years later reconfirms that observation.)

So Jesus is talking *first* to us. You have chosen to remain in the inner circle. (At least you're still reading this book!) Let us listen carefully to His next challenges.

The first challenge is to singlemindedness. Jesus says, "Be on your guard against the yeast of the Pharisees, which is hypocrisy" (v. 1). The original Greek verb is a continuing present imperative to emphasize that we must constantly be fighting hypocrisy. We will never totally get rid of it, so we must at all times guard against it.

The context of this instruction is significant. In the eleventh chapter of Luke, Jesus had called the crowds to light rather than darkness, to singleness of eye (11:33-36). Then, during a dinner party, Jesus had denounced the Pharisees in a series of several woes because of their lack of singleness. His words were harsh. Luke comments that when Jesus left the party the Pharisees and teachers of the law began to "oppose him fiercely" (11:53) and to try insidiously to catch Him at something so that they could do away with Him. Jesus had set off tons of explosives. In the glaring light, reality could be clearly seen.

Now in the twelfth chapter Jesus warns His disciples to avoid the hypocrisies of the Pharisees. Leaven, or yeast, He calls it, and the term carries the weight of profound Old Testament connotations.

In Exodus 12:14-20 we find strict instructions given to the Israelites for removal of all yeast from their homes during the Passover. Whoever ate anything with leaven in it must be cut off from the community of Israel.

Now Jesus speaks of yeast as a symbol of hypocrisy, which is just as pervasive, as constant, and as slowly penetrating. Once a person is caught up into a bit of hypocrisy it escalates profoundly. Think of some examples in your own life.

Perhaps we're all aware of the problems that various celebrities have had because of too rapid a rise to fame. Especially among Christians, there is a terrible danger of elevating well-known converts too fast—before they have time to reach maturity in their Christian life and faith. Then, when the fans expect dynamic strength in them, they must pretend in order not to disappoint. Tragically, as the pretending grows, the faith diminishes—until the celebrity wonders if any faith is really there at all.

Hypocrisy is especially insidious because inevitably we will get caught in the end. If we pretend to be what we are not, we destroy our true selves in the attempt and are miserably false in the process. Or we might get so presumptuous in our moral rectitude that we lose all sense of true right and wrong, of what really matters in life. That is what Jesus sharply rebukes in the Pharisees. They would get persnickety about tithing even their dill weed and sprigs of mint from their gardens, but meanwhile widows and orphans were suffering; injustice was rampant; worship was hollow and empty; the love of the Lord was gone from their lives.

I grew up despising the Pharisees. And then I grew up spiritually to realize that I am one of them. It is easy for me to stand on the outside of situations and condemn those involved for their terrible sins (even if I would never verbalize it like that). And then comes the rude awakening when I discover that I have done the same, but probably more so. I have been just as prejudiced, or just as cold, or just as immoral as those I condemn.

And I'm even being Pharisaical when I talk about my sins in general terms—because then I can avoid really facing them, and I can still conclude that I'm not half bad after all. And I'm sure you do the same. So let's get specific.

I need to admit that I'm a Pharisee about my moral purity. I condemn those who get involved in extra-marital sexual relationships, and yet I forget that Jesus said that our lustful thoughts are as much sin as our actual deeds of adultery. My thoughts are not always holy. I get selfish in my need for affection and fail in my relationships to build up the other person as much as I can. My sins of omission are just as sinful as those of commission.

Or perhaps I condemn those that are prejudiced against minority peoples or those who don't care about the handicapped. It is easy to get pretty proud about my supposed openness and concern. But I must face my own prejudices against those whose worship is different from mine or against those who I think are not as free from prejudice. I get very impatient with the "old-fashioned" people of the church who simply are not able to accept all the changes that I want to force upon them. Exposing my hypocrisy to you is painful, but perhaps it will encourage you to face some of your own.

Jesus says to His disciples and to us, "There is nothing concealed that will not be disclosed, or hidden that will not be made known" (v. 2). It horrifies me to realize that all my motives will be made known. All the subtle, selfish reasons for my behavior, all the aggrandizing attitudes, all my false displays of love and affection in order to meet my needs, all my hidden antagonisms will be clearly seen for what they are.

The imagery of verse 3 lays it on the line. Jesus gets more particular and says, "What you have said in the dark will be heard in the daylight, and what you have whispered in the ear in the inner rooms will be proclaimed from the housetops." He is speaking of the same sorts of things Paul refers to when he urges those who are of the light not even to speak of those things that are committed in the darkness (Eph. 5:8-12). We need to stay so far away from such behavior that we don't even speak of it.

Why is it that we don't want others to overhear our gossip? Why do children go into the kitchen in the dark to steal cookies from the jar? Obviously, we know deep down that our thoughts and attitudes and actions are sinful.

If we have a relationship that isn't exactly what it should

be, it will make us uncomfortable when we are with the person involved and uncomfortable when we try to talk to others about it. Until we confess our guilt, we will try hard to rationalize our behavior, to convince ourselves that we really are being noble or are ministering to that other person. Deep inside, however, we will know the truth. We will know that we are manipulating the other person to meet our own needs. Ultimately, Jesus says, the truth will come to light.

We can't brush the truth off with empty and pious generalizations. Even as I have been writing these paragraphs, I am terribly convicted by the facts. I have not always been truthful in relationships, and the hypocrisy of my ministry to other persons has hurt both me and them. I must confess that to them and face up to that ugliness in myself, the phoniness of my affection. That is painful to deal with, but now that I have put it down on paper the process has begun. What might this passage mean practically for you?

The inner rooms in the homes of Jesus' time were the storeroom chambers farthest away from exterior walls. When Luke uses that term combined with the fact that the messages have been whispered in the ear, we recognize how subtle hypocrisy is. How cleverly we hide our guilt and shame! How much we conceal what is really happening in our lives.

Those things, however, that were whispered in the ear in the inner rooms will be proclaimed from the housetops, Jesus warns. The flat roof would make a perfect platform. Those most secret things will be announced with the fullest publicity. There can be no more pretending.

I remember with dismay the horrible shock it was to the American public when the contents of the Watergate tapes were revealed. All the foul language and vindictive attitudes and cruel deceits were terribly different from surface appearances. Many of us experienced great grief as these evils were exposed with all the glare of national headlines.

I think I would be thoroughly shattered by this text except for the fact that it must be read with an awareness of the context in which Jesus uses the imagery. Jesus speaks of this disclosure and public manifestation in the context of encouragement to the disciples that they do not need to fear those who harm the body but are not able to kill the soul. Such beautiful words of assurance as "Indeed, the very hairs of your head are all numbered" and "Don't be afraid; you are worth more than many sparrows" (v. 7) are included in this context.

Part of the disclosure at the end, then, will be also the revelation of the truth of the discipleship of those who are committed. The character of the child of God will be revealed in its faithfulness. What was learned in the dark of one's inward study will be revealed in the light of the outward actions. What was understood in the silence of daily quiet times will be proclaimed from the rooftops.

There is great comfort in knowing that the truth of our spiritual lives will eventually be vindicated. Sometimes when I am criticized or mocked for the stands I take or the principles I try to uphold in being a child of God, I lose my courage and want to back off. But there is always this comfort: if I am faithful to what God's Word reveals to me about Him and about me, the truth of my discipleship will be proclaimed from center stage.

We have to cling to that in the tough times when we stand alone. We can't be egotistical about it because we know that such clinging, too, is only possible by the grace that enfolds us and the fact that God hangs on to us first. Once I was flunked on an exam because I interpreted a poem (written by a Catholic priest) with "too much religious exuberance." The vindication came several months later when the chairman of the graduate committee confessed to me the loneliness and pain out of which his spite had come.

God has been in charge of many situations when I didn't have the courage or the social adroitness to deal with them. Regardless of my ineptitude and fear, the God who is faithful to uphold us was revealed for who He is. What I was learning painfully in the still spaces of my life was proclaimed from the university tower.

God *is faithful!*

You might have noticed that we have come full circle back to where we started. Whether those verses indict us or comfort us depends upon whether we remain on the outside fringe or join the circle of those disciples to whom Jesus spoke first. If we join the crowds, the people who are merely the "hangers on," we will be exposed for our hypocrisy. If we are committed to this Jesus who makes such bold claims on our lives, we will be revealed in our response to His faithfulness.

That intensifies the challenge for us. Not only must we face in this chapter the challenge of His call to discipleship, but we must also recognize the eternal outcome of our choice. That should generally have a positive effect. If we would more often stop to realize the eternal dimensions of our behavior, we would choose to be more real.

These first three verses of Luke 12 lay out for us the challenge. Will we listen to the words of Jesus superficially—and, consequently, hypocritically? Or will we let them hit home deeply in our minds and souls and lifestyles? The call to commitment is a costly one. It will demand our deaths. But to choose hypocrisy will cause us to miss out on the abundant life that is available only to those who are resurrected from their deaths to become new creations in Christ Jesus. Continued hypocrisy could cause us to miss out on eternal life altogether.

It is indeed a life-or-death choice. Don't let yourself get trampled by the crowds. Jesus wants to speak to you first.

Questions for Personal Application

1. In what dimensions of my life would I rather squirm in among the crowds than take a decisive stand for Jesus?

2. In what kinds of situations have I been forced to consider the cost of discipleship?

3. How have I experienced the pervasiveness of my own hypocrisy?

4. How have I experienced the exposure of my hypocrisy?

5. What are the benefits of facing and admitting my hypocrisies?

6. How have I been vindicated in the manifestation of my faithfulness?

7. How have I experienced recently the faithfulness of God?

2 To Be the Friend of Jesus

"I tell you, my friends, do not be afraid of those who kill the body and after that can do no more."

—Luke 12:4

"So what's the worst thing that could happen?" my friend Bob demanded of me. He was helping me sort through some of my fears about my work as a free-lance speaker. I had been telling him that sometimes the financial risk worried me. What if I didn't receive enough in honorariums for the financial requirements of our EPHESUS Community? I hadn't been concerned about finances when only my salary was involved. I didn't need very much to live on, and I love ministering so much I don't really work for money. But now Christians Equipped for Ministry (CEM) has expanded. We have hired a director for the compassion and hospitality ministry of our EPHESUS house. What if I didn't bring in enough money and the whole corporation went belly up?

"So what would happen?" Bob asked again. And as I faced my ridiculous fears head-on, I realized their idiocy—especially because the CEM board of directors had repeatedly rebuked me for worrying about something that was their responsibility.

It wouldn't have been so easy to confront those fears if Bob hadn't helped me. But he is my friend, and I knew he wasn't forcing me to answer tough questions out of cruelty. His concern and care were obvious; he wanted to free me from needless worries that were impeding my effectiveness. It took a long time before the CEM board convinced me that they did indeed want to be fully responsible for all the finances of our work, but finally their love for me broke through. Why hadn't I seen before how deeply they love me, how firmly committed to this work they are?

I ask that question even more in my relationship to God. Why do I so often get so foolish as to fear elements of my human situation? Although the context of this fourth verse from Luke 12 contains a bit of law, it is primarily a lovely passage of grace. It assures us as we struggle with our perspectives that we are intimately, personally cared for by an almighty God.

Luke 12:4 is the only place in the synoptic gospels (Matthew, Mark, and Luke) in which Jesus calls the disciples "My friends." The very rarity of the expression underscores its comfort for us. That the followers of Jesus can actually be His friends is almost too good to be true. Although one of the first hymns I ever learned was "What a Friend We Have in Jesus," I still am overwhelmed every time I pause to think about the Joy such a statement creates. A basic problem with my faith life is that I don't pause often enough to realize its truth.

We learn more about the friendship of Jesus from His comments to the disciples in John 15. His beloved friend records these words for us:

> "Greater love has no one than this, that one lay down his life for his friends. You are my friends if you do what I command. I no longer call you servants, because a servant does not know his master's business. Instead, I have called you friends, for everything that I learned from my Father I have made known to you. You did not choose me, but I chose you to go and bear fruit—fruit that will last. Then the Father will give you whatever you ask in my name. This is my command: Love each other."
>
> John 15:13-17

Seven special dimensions of the qualities of our friendship with Jesus strike me in this passage. First of all, friendship with Christ involves sacrifice and commitment.

We are Christ's friends because He laid down His life to make that possible. I tried to think of some human analogy to make the impact of this fact more tangible, but I can't come up with one. It is just too incredible. The absolutely holy, incarnate God could not be friends with us as we were. His holiness separates Him so far from us in our sinfulness that He could not bear to look on us. All our greatest attempts with human language are grossly insufficient to describe the wonder of this grace. Yet, while we were still sinners, Christ died for us—His enemies—in order that He could thus transform us into friends.

The wonder of that was impressed upon me half a year ago, and a friend's words still flood me with Joy whenever I remember them. I was coming out of a time of deep depression because I had been rejected by one I loved. I didn't trust anybody, but I felt that when people got to know me well enough they would always leave me for someone else. Consequently, I misunderstood a comment that a friend had made and worried that he would desert me too.

After he had clarified for me what his original comment had meant, he added, "Marva, you need to know something. You are so afraid of rejection that you think I am going to run out on you or throw you overboard. You need to know that I am committed to our friendship. I won't reject you, but I will always talk things through with you."

I was tremendously relieved by that assurance. Later that same day, I wrote to a prisoner on death row with whom I have been corresponding and said, "Morris, you probably need to hear this as much as I did. I don't care who you are or what you have done or where you are going. I want you to know that I am committed to being your friend."

I don't deserve my friend's commitment. I don't deserve the CEM board's affirmation and support of my ministry. But their love and commitment to me certainly do make it possible to be delivered from my fears.

Similarly, there is an overwhelming freedom from fear made available to us when Jesus calls His followers friends before He bids them not to fear. The other dimensions of friendship John records are based on this initial word of sacrifice and commitment.

Second, we are the friends of Jesus if we do what He commands. There are two ways we could look at that sentence—one coming from law and one coming from gospel. If we read it as law, it would mean, "If you fall out of line and don't do what I want, you won't be my friends anymore." How terrifying such a reading is!

If we read it as gospel, Jesus is saying, "We are such good friends, and the evidence of it is that we have the same goals and purposes. You do what I command." In other words, our friendship is revealed by the fact that our deepest heart's desire is to be following His plans. I think that the context of the verse frees us for that interpretation.

Think of what a pleasure it is for you to do what your friends want. Think of the crazy things you do for someone you love. Last spring I made an afghan for one of my best friends. I don't usually sit down to do such things, but I was so excited about making it for her as an expression of my love for her that I didn't ever want to stop crocheting.

Jesus calls on this quality of friendship when He urges His followers in Luke 12 not to be afraid. And because we want to do what He commands, we try to pay attention to His instructions about not fearing our enemies.

Third, Jesus tells us in John 15 that He calls us friends because He has made known to us what He had learned from the Father. He reminds us that servants don't know their master's business. In connection with the exhortation of Luke 12 not to fear, this quality of friendship draws us into all the promises of God concerning our protection and His loving care. We don't have to worry about those that might harm our body. God is more than able to protect us from harm, and, if in His wisdom He allows us to go through painful circumstances, His grace is sufficient for all our needs (2 Cor. 12:9). He will not leave us orphaned (John 14:18). He will work all things together for our good (Rom. 8:28). He will bring us to Himself even though men might kill our bodies.

The secret lies in knowing our Master's business, and His work is to purify and fashion us. In the situation of the flunked exam described in chapter 1, I didn't understand God's purposes at first, and I was afraid. When I began to realize the kinds of exciting opportunities for ministry that came out of my situation, my fears could subside. And now, many years later, I'm still learning lessons from that whole experience. The privilege of friendship with Jesus is that He invites us into the family conclaves of the Trinity and lets us in on the secrets of the Kingdom. When we know those better, we can move more boldly and without fear.

At the conference I attended last week, I spent some time wrestling with my fears about my ministry. But in the silence of the retreat and in the affirmation of the other participants and in the clarifying of the call of God, I became so much more aware of the privilege of ministry that I felt I could tackle the world. Everyone else there felt like that too. The enormous confidence arose out of our growing friendship with Jesus in the deep devotional experiences we were having. Our theme song became this chorus from the Catholic missal: "Be not afraid; I go before you always. Come, follow Me, and I will give you rest."

We do indeed have rest from our fears when we follow Jesus. He leads us right into the Father's business as friends and not servants. By His sacrifice and commitment He has made that possible.

The fourth quality of our friendship with Jesus is that

we are chosen. It is not a question of our having chosen Him; that is not any big accomplishment on our part. He is so eminently worth choosing that it is only right to choose Him. But the fact that we are chosen is a most unexpected reality. That fact fills us with wonder and chases away fear.

It implies an incredible specialness. Think about the friends that you have chosen. You pick them because you have interests in common, because there are certain things that you like to do together, because you enjoy their company for any of a number of reasons. You choose your friends uniquely.

Isn't it amazing to realize that God wants to choose each one of us because of our specialness to Him? We choose some special friends and call them "best friends" because of the uniqueness and depth of those relationships. But a human being is capable of having only a few best friends. God, on the other hand, is able to choose each one of us to have that kind of closeness.

Think how protective you are of your best friends. It breaks our hearts when they go though sorrows. We want to protect them if we can. Three very close friends of mine are presently out of work, and it hurts me to watch them go through such struggles to find self-confidence and employment. I pray for them often every day and agonize with them over the difficulty of the long waiting time. My own behavior, out of a limited depth of love, makes me realize how much more the Father loves us, how much He must agonize with us when we are afraid, how much the fact that we are chosen affects this exhortation from Jesus not to be afraid.

The fifth quality of our friendship with Jesus is that we have been chosen by Him for that special relationship in order that we could bear fruit and, moreover, that the fruit will last. In the face of fearing those who might harm our bodies this quality of friendship is eternally comforting.

Jesus is interested in us because He has work for us to do. One of my friends, who serves in a critical area of ministry, said once, "God's going to keep me around a bit longer. There are still things for me to do."

This assurance does not give us liberty to be foolish about our lives, to enter situations of risk to which we are not called. But if we are called to tasks that involve danger to our lives, we can enter them boldly, knowing that we go out in the power of Him who has called us.

That sounds terribly abstract, but it gets delightfully practical even in small matters. I was teaching in Alaska this past August, and an old toe injury from a tennis game in July broke open and became severely infected. I don't heal well and am very susceptible to gangrene so the problem was quite worrisome. The doctor threatened to hospitalize me, but I was about to begin teaching a series of workshops on the basics of the Christian faith and on skills for doing ministry.

I asked the people in my classes in Anchorage to pray for my toe, and I sat teaching with my foot propped on a pillow. God had called me to bear fruit by teaching, so there was no place for fear of what those nasty little germs or bacteria or whatever might do to me. My toe healed surprisingly well.

The sixth quality that Jesus promises is the remarkable assurance that whatever we ask in His name the Father will give us. The fact that He lets us work in His name is an extraordinary privilege, for the biblical concept of *name* involves everything that a person is. To ask in the name of Jesus, then, implies that it is possible for us to have the mind of Christ, that we can be one with Him in His purposes and, therefore, can ask appropriately for what we need to bear fruit. That delivers us from the fear of anyone who might seem to obstruct our ministry.

I bought a lovely old five-bedroom house to aid in the ministry to single and deserted persons. I wanted to create a Christian community so filled with love that the lonely could here find encouragement and fellowship and courage. The money for the down payment on the house was given quite miraculously. (That story will be told in chapter 7.) But after we moved into the house I went through a time of tight finances in my personal accounts. One person owed me $400, and I feared his power to withhold it from me unfairly.

Finally, when I was talking over my fears with my friends John and Dianne, they asked me if I really needed the money that much. At first I wanted to say, "Yes!" but then I began to realize how extraordinary God's provision had been. I certainly did not need to fear what one person could do to me.

That night in my prayer time I finally released the matter into God's hands and asked Him to continue to provide for me according to His best purposes. I felt a calm and a peace that were so deep that I didn't even care about the money anymore. Moreover, within 18 hours of that prayerful decision I received two checks, each for $200, from two persons who had been at retreats I had led in the previous two weekends. Both of them said in essence, "These are not contributions for the CEM organization. These are for you to use personally."

And then, as if to remind me that God is able to do far more abundantly then ever we could ask or think, I received in the mail two weeks later the $400 that I was owed. I am convinced more than ever that this house and its ministry are the Lord's. If we are seeking to accomplish His purposes in this place, we can ask boldly in His name for what is needed, and the Father will provide.

It is not that we have a push-button God, who runs to fulfill our requests so that we can take life easily. No, rather it is that our friendship with Jesus draws us into the purposes of the Father, the business of the Master. Then, when He provides what we need to accomplish His good will, we will recognize His hand of blessing and not take His provisions for granted.

We certainly don't need to fear, then, anyone who threatens us with harm to our bodies. The Father will give us whatever we need, whatever we ask according to our friendship with His Son.

Finally, Jesus says that the sole command of His friendship is that we love each other. That especially gives us freedom from fear of our enemies because perfect love casts out all fear (1 John 4:18). If I am all wrapped up in loving the one who is trying to hurt me, I don't have to worry about that hurt.

I remember with great gratitude to my mother a childhood experience in which I didn't know how to handle a girl in my fourth-grade class who kept spreading bad rumors about me. My mother advised me to ask this enemy to help me pass out the invitations to the party that I was planning to hold during Christmas vacation. I thought it strange to choose my enemy for a job that made her special in fourth-graders' eyes, but that was my first exposure to the "heaping burning coals of fire" principle (Prov. 25:21-22). My mother was magnificently wise. It worked. Not only was the party more fun, but my little enemy stopped spreading the lies.

Out of our friendship with Jesus we have the resources to love those who would destroy our bodies (or spirits or minds or souls). We love because He first loved us (1 John 4:19). This last quality of Christ's friendship described in John 15 not only takes away our need to fear, but also gives us extra awareness of the possibility actually to transform the situations that cause people to be our enemies.

Aren't those seven qualities of our friendship with Jesus stupendous? If we realize their implications, we are powerfully freed to listen to His exhortation not to fear. What does it matter, He asserts, if someone might be able to destroy your body? That person has no more power. The Greek says literally, "And after these things not having a greater thing to do" (v. 4).

Anyone who can harm us physically and then can do no more does not really have very much power. That piece of truth puts a lot of things into proper perspective. It calls us to reflect upon what actually is the essential life in our existence.

Think with me about how much of our American culture reflects the philosophy that our physical existence is the essence of life. Commercials on television appeal to the pleasure of our bodies. Many of our slang expressions, such as, "If it feels good, do it," reveal the attitude that our physical comfort is the only important value. Much of the temptation to immorality in our society stems from the overaccentuation of physical intimacy as the only dimension of close relationships between persons. Paul spoke of the same misplaced emphasis when he described those whose god was their belly (Phil. 3:19) or when he declared that one of the signs of the age is that folks seek for those whose teaching merely tickles the ears (2 Tim. 4:3).

The Scriptures give us a different focus. Throughout the Word there is a distinction between the *bios,* or biological life; the *zoa,* or abundant and eternal life; and the *psyche,* or soul-life, the essence or personality. What does the body matter? One's existence is not determined by the outward tent (as Paul calls it in 2 Cor. 5:1-5). Our existence is determined by who we really are in our emotions and mind and will and spirit. Those are the centers of our relationship with God, and, as the next three verses will demonstrate, an entirely different set of values applies.

God's people can, therefore, have a totally different perspective on death from that of the rest of the world. The old philosophers urged humans to "eat, drink, and be merry, for tomorrow we die." Life had to be grabbed because it was not going to last long. Early death could be seen only as a tragedy because one had been robbed of some of his or her years (as if we had the right to them in the first place!).

For the Christian, death is another story. Several years ago when I was wrestling with the problem of death because I came close to it in my own illness, the discovery that death is not a barrier, but a door, excited me. That whole concept opened up some joyful possibilities for my understanding of both death and life.

Life is a series of barriers for which we must find ways around or through or over. Our goal is to get to God, to meet Him face to face. Various obstructions in our lives force us to choose whether we want to know Him and to fight for our relationship with Him.

The last barrier keeping us from God is this physical body. As Paul describes it in 2 Corinthians 5, what prevents us from finally being with God face to face is the limitation of this human existence. At the point of our death, that last barrier is crossed, and we can walk through the door to a perfect relationship with our Lord. That makes death for me an exciting event.

I don't want to hasten it—although, as Paul says, "I desire to depart and be with Christ, which is better by far" (Phil. 1:23). The sorrows of this world and the brokenness of people's lives make me long for the perfection of my final relationship with God. But meanwhile, He has lots of things for me to do, lots of people for me to love, lots of lessons for me to learn, lots of purifying to take place in my life.

One day, however, I will get to the last barrier. And the door through the obstacle of this physical life will be my death. What a Joy it shall be to know my Creator/Savior/Sanctifier face to face!

Until that last door, however, I will continue to live with expectation. I know that the accouterments of this existence will pass away. But the real me, my true existence, is not of the physical order. That sets me free from being bound by its needs and idiosyncrasies.

Until I reach that last door, my life is characterized by the qualities of my friendship with Jesus as described above. And the gifts of that friendship enable me to approach the last door without fear of death or of those who might cause my death. Jesus is our model. He loved those who arrested and crucified Him, and He prayed for their forgiveness. And for the Joy set before Him, He endured that cross and despised its shame. Now He is seated at the right hand of God—eternally to make friends with us.

Questions for Personal Application

1. How does Jesus' use of the phrase "my friends" personally give me comfort in the face of troubles with enemies?

2. What things am I afraid of?

3. How does my friendship with Jesus mitigate those fears?

4. Have I prepared for death in any way?

5. How does the fact of death affect the way I live?

6. How can I comfort those who are dying or those who must stand beside someone who is dying?

7. Does the "last door" picture offer me any new ways to think about death?

3 To Fear and Love God

"But I will show you whom you should fear: Fear him who, after the killing of the body, has power to throw you into hell. Yes, I tell you, fear him. Are not five sparrows sold for two pennies? Yet not one of them is forgotten by God. Indeed, the very hairs of your head are all numbered. Don't be afraid; you are worth more than many sparrows."
—Luke 12:5-7

He had only to raise his eyebrow, and I would get back in line. I loved my father so much that I wanted desperately to please him. I can remember times in my childhood when I would see him look at me sternly, and I wanted to die. I was afraid of his wrath because I knew I deserved it, and at the same time I loved him intensely. When I deserved to be punished, I would be overwhelmed with many conflicting emotions if he gave me grace instead. I was sure he was the next best thing to God.

As I grow in theological awareness, I am more and more grateful for my father. I see now how much he lives out the gospel that has molded his life. With greater maturity, I am able to see some of his faults, but they don't detract for me from the general impression of his godliness. And because he cared about me in such a holy way, I feared his wrath and loved him all the more.

There is also a proper kind of fear in our relationship with God. Jesus invites us to that healthy fear in these words from Luke 12: "But I shall suggest to you what you might fear: Fear the one having the authority after the killing to cast into gehenna. Certainly I say to you, fear this one" (v. 8, author's translation).

Such a fear is a necessary ingredient in our faith life. Those theologians who downplay the fear of God by calling it "reverence" or "respect" do us a disservice. Fear comes because we recognize the greatness and the holiness of God, the majesty and might of His separation from us and our readiness to sin. We keep getting into trouble because we make ourselves our own gods. The One who really is God has a right to be angry.

Such a fear guards against any presumption or irreverence on our part. And it also actually increases our love. When we realize how undeserving we are of God's grace and how deserving of His wrath, we are more profoundly aware of the greatness of His mercy. Jesus refers to that fact when He says that the one who is forgiven much, loves much (Luke 7:36-50).

The reason such fear is right, Jesus says, is that the One we fear has the authority to cast into gehenna. He doesn't have only the power; He also has the authority. Others might have the power to harm our bodies, but it is God's right to cast us into gehenna. We are thoroughly deserving of such judgment. No one else has the authority to condemn us. Only the One who created us in His image, the One who made everything good, the One against whom we have sinned in choosing to make ourselves our own gods, is righteous in condemning us for our choices against Him.

Most of our English translations render the Greek *gehenna* with the word *hell.* That communicates in our culture because we think in terms of the dichotomy of heaven and hell. But in the culture of Luke's day, the word *gehenna* connoted a searing picture that existed close by enough to be a constant reminder to them.

Outside the walls of Jerusalem is the Valley of Hinnom, where children had been offered to the god Molech (see the Old Testament accounts of Leviticus 18:21 and 1 Kings 11:7). In the reign of King Josiah that practice was mercifully ended (2 Kings 23:10), but the valley always carried with its name the reputation of its slaughter (see Jer. 7:32 and 19:6). In New Testament times, the valley became a garbage dump, where fires continually burned. As such, it became a symbol of punishment for those who did wrong and a graphic image of perpetual torment (Rev. 14:7-13). Our concept of hell as a place of fire and eternal pain (à la Dante) arises from the reality of the Valley of Hinnom.

Surely the punishment of God is something to be feared. But God does not deal with us on the basis of fear alone. One of the greatnesses of Martin Luther was that he discovered the scriptural balance of law and gospel. The Law was necessary to drive us to our knees, to impress us with the severity of our sin and the desperation of our existence. But when we have reached the point of shame and remorse, God's Word to us is not law but Good News, the gospel hope of grace and forgiveness, eternal and abundant life.

That is the balance in this passage from Luke 12. Immediately after Jesus tells His disciples that God is to be feared because He has the authority to dispense punishment, He reminds them again of God's infinite love and tender care. We are not doomed to be blasted. The fires of gehenna do not wait for us.

The pictures Jesus uses to show the Father's care are graphically memorable. "Are not five sparrows sold for two pennies?" Jesus asks. And yet one little one out of them all is not forgotten before God. Jesus must have used the same picture on several occasions with slight variations. Matthew records a different version, and in the difference we see the little value of these birds. Matthew 10:29 records the price of sparrow as two for a penny. The penny (*assarion* in Greek) is a very small coin; sixteen of the assarion made a denarius, which was worth about eighteen cents. But if two were sold for one penny and five were sold for two, then we realize that if a person bought double, an extra bird was thrown in for free.

"Look," Jesus is saying with a smile. "Even the one that is thrown in for free is not forgotten before God."

That is how careful He is about that which He created. If the sparrow is that important to God, how much more important are we who have been made in His image?

There were a lot of sparrows in my home town in Ohio. I remember watching them in the winter while I did my newspaper route and hearing my mother talk about how wonderful it was that they could survive in the winter. I'm sure she told me that they were a picture of God's care for His children. Similarly, in times of fear, I always felt comfort when I kept my eyes on the picture of Jesus that hung in our living room or the picture in my bedroom of Jesus and the young lad piloting a ship together in a raging storm.

It's too bad I had to grow up and get fearful. Yesterday I panicked when I discovered that the carpet in the corner of my office in the basement of this old house was soaked. I immediately wondered why I ever bought such an old place when I am incapable of fixing things. It was hard to fight the worry all day long as I waited for a friend to come over to take care of the matter. When he discovered that the problem was a leak from the bathroom immediately above my office, I should have been able to relax from my fears that the water was coming in from the outside and that the cement structure would have to be redone. And when he fixed the problem in the bathroom and lent me his space heater to dry out the carpet, I should have been freed from my worry that the new carpet would be permanently damaged. And when he stayed around to help fix a few other things in the house, I should have been enabled to realize the gracious hand of God, always providing for all of my needs. But I get so stupid and untrusting. I do not always see very clearly the perfect love of my heavenly Father, which would cast out my fear if I would recognize it.

In an age when so many people doubt their self-worth, Jesus' words are outstandingly relevant. All the philosophies that have been developed, all the psychological theories, all the techniques for affirming people, cannot compare with the reality of these comments by Jesus in their power to give us a sense of worth.

The reason is that the systems of the world base the value of a human being on the person. And if I tell a woman who has a bad image of herself that she really is a beautiful person, she probably won't believe me. If someone is convinced that he has nothing of merit to contribute to society, it will be very difficult for anyone to convince him otherwise.

But the good news from Jesus is that my worth does not depend on myself. My worth is a fact because the One who made me just as I am cares infinitely for me. Even the tiniest product of His creativity is worthy of His constant care. How much more worthy, then, are we?

I've never asked a person that I've been counseling if she thinks she's worth more than a bird, but I think I'll try that the next time it is appropriate. It seems to me to be an amazing realization that if our gracious Father invests all that care in a bird, He certainly has even more love and concern for us.

Here in Olympia we have a bad crow problem. The joke is that any driving student who successfully hits one is given an automatic A. Maybe here we should put the word *crow* into the illustration of Jesus. But as much as we would like to get rid of them, our Father does not forget them. As much as sometimes we'd like to get rid of ourselves, our Father cares for us infinitely. That is incredibly good news.

Then Jesus continues with this second picture: "Indeed, the very hairs of your head are all numbered" (v. 7). The Greek perfect verb tense used in that verse is significant. It means that once the counting has been done, it remains. In other words, God numbered all the hairs of our heads once, and now He keeps a constant check. Every time we lose or gain one, He knows and keeps the record straight.

A balding friend of mine once joked, "I don't mind at all that I am growing bald; it makes me closer to God. This way both God and I know how many hairs I have." I think his joke points out the thrust of this image.

We humans worry about so many little details of our lives—some of them even sillier than the exact count of the number of hairs on our heads. I heard once the figure that 95 per cent of the things we worry about never take place. And consider how much time we have wasted then in our anxiety over those things.

The people of Jesus' time probably thought that to count all the hairs on a person's head was an impossible task. To say that God kept an accurate count, then, underscored His omniscience and omnipotence. And to think that such wisdom and strength are immeasurably applied to take care of the littlest details of our lives is terrifically encouraging.

About ten years ago it was my privilege to speak to a congregation on the text of 1 Peter 5:7-11. I had just gotten a copy of *The Living Bible* a few weeks before and was overjoyed to read the text in that paraphrase. The King James favorite, "Casting all your care upon Him; for He careth for you," had this lovely rendition: "Let him have all your worries and cares, for he is always thinking about you and watching everything that concerns you."

At that time there was an advertisement for Wind Song perfume that pictured a young man gazing thoughtfully at an image in his mind. The ad proclaimed, "He can't get you out of his mind." I was delighted with the discovery and titled my message, "Wind Song." The Spirit-wind song of God is that He can't get us out of His mind. He is always thinking about us, always watching over everything that concerns us. What infinite comfort that provides!

While I was on the retreat last week there were some times when the signs of God's overwhelming care were unbelievably frequent. Especially on the day of silence I saw gift after gift to remind me of God's faithfulness. The sun shone brightly; the leaves were flaming red and gold; the leader of the retreat read excerpts from writings that reflected exactly what I had just been thinking; he played my most favorite piece of music during lunch; and at sunset the sky turned gloriously pink, which is to me (because it is used that way liturgically) a sign of Joy. All day long, it seemed, every little thing that happened was a new sign of God's love and grace. No one else could have planned so many of my favorite things, so many exquisite experiences, such profoundly applicable lessons, so glorious a sky, such relevant insights.

On the more practical level, God's particular care for the specifics of our concerns is so precise it is baffling. For example, He constantly makes possible for me all the details of my trips to teach in various churches. I do not own a car. I have a driver's license, but because of my cataracts I am not able to drive in the dark. Yet every weekend I have the rides I need. Someone lends me a car, someone else lends me a bed if I have to stay overnight because I can't return in the dark, someone picks me up at the bus station, or someone else takes care of me while I have a layover somewhere. One weekend I had rides with eleven different persons to teach in several places. And in the midst of those provisions, so many interesting persons have become my friends, and I have felt so deeply loved and cared for. Perhaps the illustration of Jesus put into modern terms for my experiences would say, "Even the miles of your speaking trips are numbered." How would you put His illustration into your life's vocabulary?

Once again Jesus returns to the sparrows to sum up the message of His two illustrations: "Don't be afraid; you are worth more than many sparrows." The Greek sentence ends with the words about greater value. This should be the last thing in our minds as we close this chapter: our greater value.

None of us is very good at measuring our own value. We have poor self-concepts in most cases, and often we cover them up with blatant egotism. Or we cower in fear and continually put ourselves down.

From Jesus comes the grand invitation to recognize our worth—not to elevate ourselves falsely, but to be true to ourselves boldly, knowing that the way we've been put together is very, very special.

Notice the balance of law and gospel. Jesus warned us at the beginning of this section to fear the One who has the authority to cast us into gehenna. But when we take that warning seriously and fear properly the wrath of God, we are driven to grace. Then we begin to see the infinite love of a Father who watches over everything that concerns us. That vision enables us to listen to the encouragement to be not afraid. The gospel frees us from the fear of the law.

This section contains a tremendous progression of thought. We who are deserving of God's wrath, over whom He has the authority to throw us into gehenna, are called into worthiness by His care.

Questions for Personal Application

1. In what ways do I fear God?

2. In what ways do I not have to fear Him?

3. How do I see the tension of fear and love in other places in the Scriptures?

4. How does love cast out fear?

5. What image would I use to describe God's infinite care for me?

6. How does the knowledge that I am worthwhile to God affect my life-style?

7. How does His affirmation of my worth affect my attitudes?

4 The Use of Our Tongues

> *"I tell you, whoever acknowledges me before men, the Son of Man will also acknowledge him before the angels of God. But he who disowns me before men will be disowned before the angels of God. And everyone who speaks a word against the Son of Man will be forgiven, but anyone who blasphemes against the Holy Spirit will not be forgiven. When you are brought before synagogues, rulers and authorities, do not worry about how you will defend yourselves or what you will say, for the Holy Spirit will teach you at that time what you should say."*
>
> *—Luke 12:8-12*

He had hurt me deeply. He was a pastor with whom I had tried to work closely for a long time. But some of his actions toward me and the things that he said about me to others revealed the intensity of his dislike. Finally, I had to confront him. We could not work together if such hostility existed.

He told me how he felt about me and why he disagreed with my understanding of ministry. He thought that my enthusiasm "forced people to do things they weren't capable of doing." (Since my goal in ministry is to equip others, I thought that was a compliment.) I confessed to him my bitter attitudes; I was truly sorry that I had reacted defensively. I asked for his forgiveness and was shocked when he ignored my request with a wave of the hand. I was ready to forgive him and eager to restore the relationship. He didn't want my forgiveness. The relationship could not be restored.

Many people find the above paragraph from Luke 12 very difficult to understand. Why is it that blasphemy against the Son of Man, Jesus, can be forgiven, but blasphemy against the Holy Spirit is the unforgivable sin? The reason for the difference is illustrated by my relationship with the pastor described above. I could not forgive him because he did not want my forgiveness. Even so, a person who resists the Holy Spirit's gift of forgiveness and faith cannot be restored to a relationship with God.

This difficult passage is made more accessible to us also by noticing its context. The whole section from verse 8 to verse 12 describes the relationship between what goes on with our tongues here on earth and what goes on in heaven.

Although often it seems that God is far off, away in a distant heaven, that section underscores the close relationship between this world and the supernatural one. God is intensely involved in both.

Like the section discussed in the previous chapter, this passage is a combination of warning and words of encouragement. The interplay between the two is important so that we can know in the text what is the Word of God that is spoken to us. Martin Luther was extremely sensitive to the problem of people's becoming discouraged by hearing the Law when what they needed to hear was the gospel. When asked by a friend about a passage, he had the freedom to answer, "Yes, it is the word of God—but I do not think that it is the word of God to me."[1]

All of us need to hear the warnings in the words of Jesus, but we do not need to load ourselves with extra guilt by being afraid of His denial of us. Let us pay close attention together to each of the elements of this set of comments about the use of our tongues.

First, we have Jesus' strong word of assurance that if we confess Him in front of men, He Himself will confess us before the courts of heaven. The assurance is deepened by His introductory formula, "But I say to you." He adds the entire weight of His immense credibility to the promise. Because He has demonstrated perfect faithfulness to His

[1] Krister Stendahl, *Paul Among Jews and Gentiles* (Philadelphia: Fortress, 1976), p. 75.

Word, we can know for sure that He will do what He says. Never has He broken a promise yet. There is no reason whatever for us to doubt in the slightest that He will fulfill this pledge.

His comment means that there are eternal issues involved in a person's reaction to Jesus. The one who responds to His invitation with acknowledgment will, in turn, be acknowledged before the angels. Some translations render the Greek word *homologeo* as "confess"; the New International Version, which is quoted at the head of this chapter, uses the word *acknowledge.* The verb means literally, "speaking the same." The promise declares, then, that if we speak the same as Jesus—that is, if we enter into His purposes and message—He will speak the same in defense of us before the angels of God.

I don't think the latter is limited only to the final judgment, but I'm sure it definitely means that. When believers are finally separated from unbelievers, those who have been part of His Kingdom on earth will assuredly be part of His Kingdom in heaven. I think, though, that Jesus is also confessing us even now before the angels. "All the angels in heaven above rejoice when there's a soul saved." That sentence from the chorus of a song keeps ringing through my mind with great Joy as I work on this chapter. What fun they must have in heaven rejoicing when you and I confess Jesus before men!

Jesus calls Himself the Son of Man in this passage. That phrase does not exist in every one of the early manuscripts of Luke. If it was part of the original gospel account, it refers to that splendid chapter in Daniel in which the Son of Man appears before the Ancient of Days and to Him is given "authority, glory and sovereign power; all peoples, nations and men of every language worshiped him." The dominion, furthermore, "is an everlasting dominion that will not pass away, and his kingdom is one that will never be destroyed" (Dan. 7:14). In other words, Jesus brings an immense authority to His testimony concerning us before the courts of heaven. Surely what He says about us will be accepted there, and we will be recognized as His people.

In Matthew 13:36-43 the angels are pictured as being the servants of God in the final process of judgment. This Jewish concept of the angels, superior to humans in their relationship with God, underlies Jesus' use of the image of the angels of God as the ones who will listen to His acknowledgment of those of us who have confessed Him before men.

I know that Jesus will be faithful to His side of the covenant. Now the thrust of this text as I take it into my daily life must be the challenge to be always acknowledging Jesus before others. That signifies His lordship in my life. Will I let Him be the Master in everything? Will I let Him rule in every dimension of my existence?

There is a lovely little booklet from InterVarsity Press called *My Heart—Christ's Home*. The allegory of a man's house describes the lordship of Jesus. The owner didn't want Jesus to go into certain closets and rooms because they were not cleaned up yet. But Jesus wants to go into every corner of our existence and do the cleaning Himself. He wants to be Lord over everything.

That is not to be a threat to us. It is an invitation, for surely all those things that are turned over to His lordship are most effectively in our hands. We are happiest in those dimensions of our life that are perfectly in line with the will of God. When we step outside His purposes into our desires and plans, we will find ourselves frustrated and dissatisfied. What a privilege it is that Jesus invites us to acknowledge Him, to seek His lordship in everything that we are and do and think and say and become!

On the other hand, the one who denies Jesus before men will be denied before the angels of God. Lest we worry about that sentence, we must pay close attention to the verb tenses in the original Greek. The description of the one denying Him is a present tense participle; that means that the verb emphasizes continuing action. It does not refer to a single instance of denial or perhaps several ones scattered or periods of backsliding. It means, rather, that such denial is a continuous state of affairs. It is not a matter of words, but of life-style. The apostle Paul records the same emphasis in this hymn in 2 Timothy:

"If we died with him,
  we will also live with him;
if we endure,
  we will also reign with him.
If we disown him,
  he will also disown us;
if we are faithless,
  he will remain faithful,
  for he cannot disown himself."

2 Timothy 2:11-13

If we disown Him, as the final outcome of a life of resistance, He is forced by our action to deny us. But even if we are faithless and slip away from our commitment to Him and our desire for His lordship, He will remain faithful to us. He cannot go against His own character, and that character is to be faithful.

When I was going through a terribly deep time of depression because of personal crisis last year, I told my pastor that I wondered if I might fall away from my faith. I cried out against the difficulty of trusting God in such painful circumstances. I will never forget my pastor's answer. He proclaimed to me boldly, "Marva, you may let go of God's hand. But He will never let you go." I have said that to myself over and over in the times of despair: "He will not let me go." It was profoundly comforting.

Thus, this word in Luke 12 about the Son of Man denying someone before the angels of God does not apply to me. I do not need to fear that because I have had some times of doubt and despair I will not be acknowledged by

Jesus. He is indeed issuing a stern warning, but once that has been heeded in my life, I need no longer let it haunt me.

It is an important word of motivation for ministry, moreover. I know some people who are still thoroughly resisting the invitation of Jesus to acknowledge Him as Lord. I long for them to come to the point of confessing Him. I want to be as useful as possible in introducing them to the reality of the gospel. I know that Jesus wants them to acknowledge Him even more than I do. His desire is for all to be saved and to come to the knowledge of the truth (1 Tim. 2:4). But He will not cram heaven down the throat of anyone who doesn't want it. If someone persists in his disowning of Jesus, He will have to accept their refusal and disown them, too.

I'm sure that Jesus was aware as He spoke these words that His disciples would at various points turn against Him. It gives us another glimpse of His infinite compassion and tender care for His followers that His next words are the comforting assurance that everyone who speaks a word against the Son of Man will be forgiven. Surely after Peter had denied his Lord, he must have remembered this assurance that even his sin could be forgiven.

Just today I recognized something in the Greek pronouns of this section that I had never noticed before when preparing my lectures on Luke. In the two phrases that speak positively of Jesus' acknowledgment of those who confess Him and of His forgiveness of those who speak against Him, the Greek pronouns say, "Each whoever." But in the two negative comments about those who deny and those who blaspheme against the Holy Spirit, there is no pronoun. Instead, the simple article *the* before the participles says literally, "The one denying" and "the one having blasphemed." That subtle difference in grammatical construction underscores for me the grace of this passage. Everyone who speaks against Jesus Christ will be forgiven.

The sin that is forgivable is a matter of speaking a word against the Son of Man. Probably such a word is spoken out of a failure to understand who He is, or, as in the case of Peter, a misunderstanding of the power that is available to those who believe in Him. For whatever the reason, our words of ignorance and confusion and mistrust will be forgiven.

That frees me to be real about the state of my mind or soul or heart. There are times when I doubt or fear or get angry. It does not help in such a state for me to be false with Jesus and speak pious words that I cannot believe. The Psalms give us models for being real in such situations.

Notice Psalm 13 especially. Within six verses of crying out, "How long, O Lord, how long?" (v. 1), the psalmist came to the point of saying, "But I trust in your unfailing love; my heart rejoices in your salvation. I will sing to the Lord, for he has been good to me" (vv. 5-6). That is an incredible movement of spirit. But it is in keeping with the constant message of the Scriptures. There is forgiveness with Jesus, and, as a result, we can come from our griefs and doubts and despairs to the point of trusting Him once again.

What makes all that possible is the *fact* that He is *faithful* to His character. He cannot deny Himself, Paul wrote in that hymn to Timothy. Even when we are faithless, He remains faithful, for He cannot deny who He is in His constant love for us.

After the assurance of His grace in this promise of forgiveness, Jesus does remind His disciples that blasphemy against the Holy Spirit cannot be forgiven. Once again, however, we can remember that this word of warning is not a word to terrify us. Once as a child I worried excessively that I might fall away from my faith. I think it was my father who answered me, "As long as you are worrying about it, you are OK." What he meant was that as long as I was concerned about my relationship with

Jesus, I could be sure that that relationship was in fact existent.

I think that one of the terrible failures of the church is its inability to deal sensitively with people who are asking questions. Just the other night I met with a man who has all sorts of questions about how we can know that the truth is in Christ. I'm glad that he is honest about his searching. I think that the combination of Jesus' words about forgiveness for speaking against Him and His warning of no forgiveness for blasphemy against the Holy Spirit makes clear the position that we should have toward those who have doubts.

Too often when we deal harshly with those who have doubts, we drive them from the state of having words against Jesus to the position of those whose hearts are hardened into blasphemy against the Holy Spirit. The love of Christ is made known through its incarnation in His people. When they don't have enough love to deal gently with those who are searching, they fail to reveal a Jesus who is tenderly concerned about each person's understanding of who He is. When a person with honest doubts is not enabled to know the love of Christ in the midst of those doubts, he often gives up on the church and religion and feels it is utterly futile to try to get satisfactory answers. I don't think that he is giving up on Christ because he has never really had the chance yet to know Him.

I know a girl who was kicked out of a church for asking too many questions. Fortunately, she didn't let that stop her search. What a tragedy it would have been if she had allowed herself to get bitter and turn away from the truth into blasphemy against the Holy Spirit in a denial of faith.

We each must look at this warning of Jesus very carefully. We want to make sure that our hearts are open to the message of the Holy Spirit—to His call to repentance, His offer of forgiveness and salvation, His gift of faith that draws us into the lordship of Christ. And we want to make sure that our hearts are open to people, so that we are always seeking to help them be receptive, too, to the gifts of the Holy Spirit. How can we be useful to others in such warning and encouragement? How can we give them space to ask their questions and encouragement to pursue their understanding of Christ and to confront their doubts and fears until they can come to the point of acknowledging Him before others?

Before we leave this section, I need to make one more comment about the contrast between acknowledging and denying, speaking a word against, and blaspheming. There is one sort of denying and blaspheming in our times that is especially troubling to me. Leon Morris quotes another commentator's concern about the same issue in these words from his commentary on Luke:

> Moorman reminds us that there is more than one way of denying Jesus. These days, he thinks, we are unlikely to deny Him in the same way as Peter, for example, did. But we may deny 'the unique authority of his teaching, imagining that, on some points, we know better than he did, or that much of what he said can be explained away'. We may also deny His divinity and repudiate His claims. 'In either case it is the sin of pride and self-assurance, man's . . . ultimate denial of the supremacy of Christ and of God.[2]

We live in a difficult age for biblical scholarship. It seems that so much of modern biblical scholarship elevates man's mind over the authority of God. To question the validity of the Scriptures is to question God's authority and authorship of the Word. I worry not only that such scholarship is oftentimes destructive to the faith of unknowledgeable believers, but also about the state of the scholars' faith. Who am I to judge? But I must be aware in my own biblical study lest I get unfaithful and fail to acknowledge who Jesus is before those I seek to serve with my scholarship.

[2] Leon Morris, *The Gospel According to St. Luke* (Grand Rapids: Eerdmans, 1974), p. 210.

Now we come again to a word of promise. Notice that each word of warning in this section has been surrounded with messages of grace. Jesus now tells us about another dimension of the correlation between what is happening on earth and what goes on in heaven. He assures His followers that when they are brought before synagogues, rulers, and authorities, they do not have to worry about how they will defend themselves or what they will say.

The synagogues were not only places of worship and instruction in the Jewish faith. They were also the lower courts in the land. This whole paragraph in Luke 12 has been concerned for the disciples' behavior in times of persecution and opposition, but now specifically Jesus tells them how things will go when they are taken into court for being His followers.

"Rulers and authorities" might signify higher courts in the Jewish system, but Jesus could also be anticipating the Roman rule under which Christians would be persecuted in the near future. When the disciples are brought before any kind of court in order to answer to charges arising against their faith, they do not need to be anxious about how they will defend themselves. This last phrase in the original Greek carries connotations of a formal legal defense. "Do not have anxiety" about how to do that, Jesus urges. That phrase means to avoid being distracted. In other words, do not panic.

We all know what happens to us when we panic. If we are taking an exam, and we panic because it seems that we don't know any of the answers, all possibility for thinking clearly is lost. Only in a state of calm can the mind retrieve what is stored away in it. Similarly, in our defense of our faith sometimes we get so distracted about how we should answer an opponent that we do not have the calm necessary for the Holy Spirit to bring to our remembrance what we know so that we can answer.

Neither our style of defense nor its content should worry

us, furthermore. Don't worry about the *how* or the *what*, Jesus commands. The way in which we answer will be the result of the love of God that fills our lives as we grow closer to Him, and the content of our answer revolves around the character of the God in whom we believe.

Jesus expands on this promise in Luke 21:12-19. There He promises "words and wisdom that none of your adversaries will be able to resist or contradict" (v. 15). If we take that promise seriously, we will have available to us an incredible amount of power.

It grieves me that too often we Christians don't answer our challengers out of those limitless resources promised by Jesus. His plan is for us to be equipped to speak of Him so gloriously that the world around us will see His radiance. Instead of relying on our own resources, we need simply to stand firm (and tactful and joyful and loving and other such good things), knowing that truth is on our side.

It is great fun, don't you think, to debate with somebody when we know that we are right. God does not need our defense. He desires only for us to be the means by which He is introduced to those who are resisting His message of grace. Therefore, we can have great confidence in speaking of Him to others no matter what the situation.

When I was an English teacher at the University of Idaho, it was my great privilege to talk with lots of students who were searching after the truth of Christianity. I used to love especially to debate with atheists. God has assured us that He will give us the words to say. Sometimes He gave me words to admit that I didn't know the answer to a question or challenge. And when that happened, it usually turned out to be a good thing. Then I could offer to try to find out, and my atheist friend would have to come back again so that we could discuss the matter further.

One day especially stands out in my memory above all the times students came to the office to ask questions. I was teaching "Literature of the Bible" at the time and had in my class several so-called atheists whose views challenged everybody and forced the namby-pamby Christians to take a better look at their faith. We had some outstanding discussions in those classes. On that special day, a searching student whom I had never met came to the office door and said, "You don't know me, but my fraternity brother told me that I could find God in this office."

That put everything into the right perspective. My purpose in being there was merely to direct those who came to the God who was already there to be found. I could only rejoice in the privilege. I didn't have to be worried about what to say or how to say it. I knew the God who was there, and He wanted to make Himself known to others through me. He was indeed always faithful to His promises; the Holy Spirit kept teaching me what to say.

One final point about the Spirit's instruction: it will be given to us "at that time" (v. 12). That does not mean we don't need any preparation. Perhaps you've been exposed to a person who said that the Holy Spirit inspired his sermons—and they were terrible sermons because he hadn't done any work on them. The Holy Spirit does indeed give us what to say, but He makes use of the Scripture we have stored in our hearts and the lessons we have learned in our growth in faith. He requires our faithfulness and gives us the responsibility. The key is in the words, "do not worry" (v. 11). Our preparations should not cause us distraction. We shouldn't be so worried about what we will say that we prepare with agitation and dread. We shouldn't be kept from other ministry in the meanwhile because we are uptight about how we will defend ourselves.

I recall one incident in which I needed to make a clear presentation of the gospel as part of my defense for some behavior that had offended another person. I thought and worried and fretted and stewed about how I would answer her hostility. When the situation came, however, I was so overcome with love for her in her own fears and tensions that I forgot completely the little speech I had planned to make and told her simply how much I cared for her, how sorry I was that I had offended her, and how much the good news of forgiveness in Jesus Christ meant to me. Much better! My little speech would not have been effective at all.

I think this promise from Jesus is best understood when we realize that He is calling us to be real with the situation of the moment. "At that time" the Spirit will teach us what to say. We will be sensitive to the environment, to the feelings of those to whom we are speaking, and to the reality of the gospel in our lives—and our speech will flow accordingly.

The wrong kind of preparation prohibits our being real. If we believe that God wants to speak through us in our relationships with others, we will want to use His wisdom, and His words, and His love. Those are the gifts that the Spirit will convey. And He can convey them to us much more thoroughly if we are not in such a state of panic that we cannot receive His instruction.

The choices of this paragraph from Luke 12 are ours: to acknowledge or to disown, to question or to blaspheme, to worry or to be available for the Spirit to give us the words and means for defending our faith. The choices that we make here on earth are vitally connected to heavenly effects. Let us always remind each other that the God to whom we respond is faithful in His grace to us. And let's keep our ears open to hear perhaps the rejoicing of the angel choirs.

Questions for Personal Application

1. What does it mean for Jesus to be the Lord of our lives?

2. What experiences have I had acknowledging Jesus

before others and what were the outcomes?

3. How can I distinguish in the Word of God between that which does and that which does not apply to me?

4. How is the forgiveness of Jesus communicated to me? How do I know I am forgiven? (This question is designed specifically to help us confront the fact that forgivenss is a fact and not a feeling.)

5. Have I experienced some times when the Holy Spirit taught me at the proper instant what I was to say?

6. How do I react when all He teaches me is to be silent?

7. How does panic prevent ministry?

5 Not Grasping for Authority and Avoiding Covetousness

"Someone in the crowd said to him, 'Teacher, tell my brother to divide the inheritance with me.'

"Jesus replied, 'Man, who appointed me a judge or an arbiter between you?' Then he said to them, 'Watch out! Be on your guard against all kinds of greed; a man's life does not consist in the abundance of his possessions.' "

—Luke 12:13-15

I laughed at the presumption of the man in that story. And then I realized that I am just like him. I remember lots of incidents from my childhood when I was upset with my brothers. I was the youngest in the family and the only girl, and I felt that my two older brothers always picked on me unfairly. So I would go to my parents and say, "Dad, please tell Glen to give me the baseball mitt," or "Mom, make Phil do his share of the dishes." I always *knew* beforehand what the only fair judgment could be in the feuds that rose between us. I was, of course, the innocent victim of all the fights.

Now I look at my self-centeredness in all those squabbles, and I realize that I owe my brothers countless apologies. But I owe my parents even more, because I made their job of parenting even more difficult than it should have been, by not letting them really do what they were called to do. I was in reality trying to manipulate them to decide in my favor.

The problem is even more noticeably destructive in a classroom. When quarreling students demand that their teacher settle their disputes, they prevent him from doing what he is really called to do—to instruct them, to teach them principles of living that will prevent such selfishness.

That is what the man from the crowd did to Jesus, although he was observing the customary habit in Jewish society. Rabbis and lawyers (teachers of the Mosaic Law) were appealed to for settlement of disputes in that society. Particular questions of inheritance, such as the one raised by the petitioner in this story, would be settled on the basis of Jewish laws of succession, such as those given in Numbers 27:1-11 and Deuteronomy 21:15-17.

The fact that this man came to Jesus to request such an intervention reveals the way the people who surrounded Jesus must have perceived Him. This man thought that Jesus was a typical Jewish rabbi and must have been quite surprised when Jesus reacted as He did.

Jesus reacted with anything but tenderness. "Man," He said. The term implies a distance; the guy was a stranger. But the question that Jesus asks reveals the reason for His ire. "Who appointed me a judge or an arbiter between you?" (v. 14).

The form of the question teaches us two significant things about the ministry of Jesus. First of all, its form copies that of the two Hebrew men who, when fighting and stopped by Moses in the Egyptian capital, asked him who had appointed him to be judge or arbiter over them Exod. 2:14 and described similarly by Stephen in Acts 7:27). The Hebrew men didn't accept Moses' authority over them when he wanted to exert it. Jesus, to the contrary, wouldn't accept that kind of authority over men when they wanted to submit to it from Him.

It would have been nice for His ego. He could have accepted that position and received the favor of men. But Jesus, even though He actually was God and deserved to be recognized as the authority and judge in all cases of human experience, did not think equality with God a thing to be grasped. Instead, He emptied Himself and became a servant—to men, but, even more important, to God's plan that He humble Himself all the way to the point of death (see Phil. 2:5-11).

And that is the second critically important lesson that we

learn from this little incident. Jesus would not accept that authority because it was not part of the Father's plan for the salvation of the world. He couldn't waste time doing things that were not part of His call. Certain tasks were His top priorities, and He would not be dissuaded from them.

That was the secret of His power and the perfect effectiveness of His ministry. He did only those things that the Father wanted Him to do. Notice how often in the gospel of John Jesus makes that claim. Repeatedly, He says such things as, "This command I received from my Father" (John 10:18b) or "My food . . . is to do the will of him who sent me and to finish his work" (4:34) and so forth.

These two lessons say armloads to us about our ministries. Jesus is, of course, the perfect model for us. Our lives are to follow His pattern. The first letter of Peter says that Jesus suffered for us to leave us an example—literally, a pattern to trace—that we should follow in His steps (1 Pet. 2:21).

Notice that this little incident in the midst of a crowd probably caused some suffering for Jesus. He suffered in giving up His pride; He did not accept the praise of men by going along with their proposals for His use of time. Further, He suffered because He no doubt raised their ire when He refused to judge this case. And especially He must have angered them by the way in which He went on: "Be on your guard against all kinds of greed" (v. 15). What a put-down!

The man who had asked for His judgment in the case against his brother was being told that Jesus would not cater to his covetousness. That is a pretty strong rebuke. Jesus must have suffered also some misunderstanding in this scene. And later He was to suffer the misunderstanding of the whole society as they raised their voices in angry opposition to His entire life and teaching. "Crucify Him," they screamed, and the venom of their cries was violent poison to His sensitive spirit.

So now what about us? These two lessons can be applied to our servanthood, our sense of ministry and mission. First of all, the story warns us against any sort of grasping for authority or power not appropriate to our calling. We want always to keep before us the nature of our discipleship: we have the mind of Christ so that we can be like Him in laying aside any authority not in keeping with the humbling to servanthood that a life in Him requires.

Second, we need to accept with Joy the suffering that might be entailed in sticking to our principles. Our ministry will be much more focused if we can follow the first lesson and do only the things to which we are called. But it will involve more misunderstanding, some struggle, piercing pain.

I'm sure that some of you are wondering, "But how do I know what it is that I am called to? How can I find the proper authority in my ministry when I'm working in a job that I don't like? I have to work somewhere to survive."

One of the residents of our EPHESUS Community wrestles with those questions right now. She has great artistic gifts, but has to work in a secretarial job in order to have a paycheck. How do these lessons apply to someone like her?

I don't want to be glib about these very painful struggles. I realize how fortunate I am that I can do work that uses my gifts and is very enjoyable to me. But I am also beginning to learn what kinds of struggles and sufferings any work involves, especially for those whose work is not what they would choose.

For those of you who are not in careers that use your gifts of ministry, one of the sufferings to which you might be called is that very real sense of wasted time. Perhaps your life's work can't give you the Joy of being able to serve the Lord more directly with your gifts. But through the suffering of serving in a very humble way in a job that doesn't fulfill you, you might have opportunity to minister to many who suffer from the same meaninglessness and don't know the power of Jesus to give life its purpose. Perhaps your calling is to be sensitive to that frustration, to be an exhorter to the countless people who hate their work and need to find some healing in it.

Perhaps, then, the first lesson will become even more real to you. You cannot accept a power that you might crave. But in setting aside any authority extraneous to your calling, you will be empowered to serve so much more effectively in the humility of the boring job. Your Joy in ministry, then, might be found in the liberality with which you can give away your financial resources, or in the quiet conversations that might dot your break times, or in the power of the prayers that you can be making throughout your day's work.

I'm eager for you to explore in your quiet times the ways in which these two lessons might apply to your particular work situation. Perhaps you might want to pause right now to think about that for a while before continuing with this chapter.

I paused, too, and checked out what I had just written with my housemates. We talked together of the importance of these questions of discipleship. We cannot give each other final answers about the meaning of our work or how we find the will of God for our lives, especially in regard to our jobs and ministries. But we can encourage each other to wrestle with these questions of the faith, to desire always a deeper discipleship. Together we can explore what kinds of authority we must lay aside and what kinds of suffering we must undergo in order that we do not take to ourselves an authority that is not in keeping with the calling that is particular for each one of us. If you belong to some sort of prayer- or caring- or mission-group, perhaps you might talk together about these questions. If you don't belong to any, now might be the time to begin such a group so that you can have fellow Christians with whom to share deeply in the struggles of a more committed and more effective discipleship.

We must ask at this point what the job is to which Jesus was committed that would cause Him to turn aside this request for Him to be an arbiter. As we skim through the synoptic gospels (which look from essentially the same perspective on events), we hear Jesus constantly talking about the Kingdom of God.

We will look much more closely in later chapters at the nature of His Kingdom and the characteristics of His kingship, but for now it will suffice for us to be aware of the whole texture of our lessons from Luke 12. We have seen already Jesus' comments concerning our acknowledgment of Him, and the fact that His Spirit will teach us what to say, and the need for us always to be on our guard against any form of hypocrisy in His Kingdom. Now once again, Jesus uses the expression of being on our guard against another dangerous element that wants to creep into discipleship. He moves immediately away from the man's request by telling him and all of us that we must avoid greed to be part of His Kingdom.

"Watch out and be constantly on your guard against all kinds of covetousness," His warning says literally in the Greek text. The two verb forms create an interesting forcefulness. The first is an aorist imperative—a once-and-for-all, "Watch out!" The second is a present continuing middle imperative—"Keep being on guard to yourselves." It is as if Jesus were saying to that man, "Look out to what is happening right now, and then continue to go on watching at all times for all the kinds of covetousness that will catch you if you are not careful."

There is a very great seriousness in that warning. Right now we must look to the covetousness of our lives. And for the rest of our time in this existence we need to be guarding ourselves against the many kinds of greed that would pull us away from the Kingdom. Covetousness violates our relationship with God.

The use of the middle verb is significant. In Greek, it is halfway between the active mood, "watch out," and the passive mood, "be watched out for," so it means literally, "watch out for yourselves." It implies that there is positive action that we can take in order to avoid covetousness.

That means, for example, that I don't go to shopping centers unless it is necessary. Window shopping just creates in me desires for things that I think I might want, although I usually don't care all that much about clothes. I very much don't want to stir up longings for possessions I don't need. My money is committed to caring for the poor of the world who don't have a fraction of what I possess. Sin is cleverly subtle, however. Since I don't go shopping, I am not ordinarily deceived into much covetousness along that line.

But I get greedy about books instead. Or sometimes I get covetous for experiences. While I was teaching, my housemate Julie left a conference that she was attending with me to have lunch with some mutual friends of ours. I wanted to go with them, too, but knew that I needed to stay to minister to those who might want individual help. I had to battle with that coveting of the fun instead of doing my work. It helped to confess my envy to Julie and to hear a reminder that I am forgiven.

See how pervasive covetousness is? That is why Jesus says, "Keep being on guard for yourselves against *all kinds* of covetousness." What kinds of things or experiences do you covet?

Consider your desires for power or prestige or popularity. What about my need for affirmation, my desires to possess my friends' fellowship or their time, or my greediness for experiences that will make me feel good? Do I covet someone else's privileges, or sense of perfect pitch, or abilities for ministry, or knack for keeping a clean house?

Do you see all the subtle ways that we are snagged into the greed of this man who wanted a larger share of the inheritance? He probably was the younger son and wanted more than he deserved by Jewish law. His brother most likely was the eldest, who was entitled to twice as much as his brothers. Do we similarly question God's division of the inheritance and wish that we had been given a larger share of the gifts in the Body of Christ or a larger portion of the responsibility or a bigger slice of the glory? Against all kinds of covetousness we need to be constantly on our guard.

I think that one of the most dangerous tools of Satan for increasing our covetousness is the television set. The commercials we observe are intended to stir up in us wants —for bigger and better and more things, for the good life, for comfort and pleasure. I don't see anywhere in Christ's words about the Kingdom the instruction that as the King's children we should seek the good life.

Jesus goes on to stress that. He presents to the covetous man and to us this principle of life: that it does not consist in the overflowing to us of an abundance of possessions. We will never find true life in the accumulation of stuff. That is an important rebuke to each one of us in this age of affluence.

Jesus had pulled away from the job the man wanted to impose on Him for the same reason the apostles appointed almoners in Acts 6—not to ignore questions of social justice, but so that they could concentrate on the proclamation of the Kingdom. Now as He declares that life does not consist in the gathering of an abundance of possessions, He begins His instructions concerning discipleship and material things, especially money. Many more of His instructions as we study them from Luke 12 will involve questions of the stewardship of finances. Here we first begin to catch the flavor of His teaching. This basic principle starts us out in our quest for better commitment of our money to the purposes of the Kingdom of God.

We must learn that our life does not consist in what we have. There are two sides to the dangers of greed. On the one hand, it causes us to aim at the wrong things in life, the physical objects that we think will satisfy our terrible cravings. On the other hand, avarice pulls us away from what really matters, our relationship with God, who alone can satisfy the longings that haunt us.

C.S. Lewis talks about those longings in terms of the German word *Sehnsucht.* I have discussed this more at length in my first book, *To Walk and Not Faint,* so I won't say much about it here, but the problem of that terrible longing is the root of the danger against which Jesus warns here.

Lewis says that we have an inexplicable longing for something in our lives, and we don't know how to satisfy it. If we think that possessing things can still that restlessness in us, we will fall into the fool's way of hopping from one inadequate goal to another. When we reach one goal, such as buying a new car, we soon discover that it has not filled that aching void in our lives. So we set a new goal, like buying a house, or taking an expensive vacation, or changing to a new major in college, or starting to work because we think that we are unfulfilled as a homemaker.

But none of those things will be sufficient. Any greed or any sin will turn to dust in our mouths as we discover more and more the painful reality of the ineffectiveness of things to satisfy our deepest desires.

The great saint Augustine told us how to keep our values straight when he described the answer to this insatiable *Sehnsucht* in our lives. We can only cry out, "Oh, Lord, Thou hast made us, and our spirits are restless until we find rest in Thee."

Lately I have caught in myself a strange new kind of

covetousness that is hard to confess. And yet I realize that it can too easily rob me of the real meaning of life and wholeness. I get greedy for experiences of comforting. When I get scared of the responsibility of my work, I desire intensely for someone to hold me and tell me that everything is going to be all right, that I am loved, that I can be strengthened by that affirmation to get back into ministry and serve some more.

True life does not consist in the abundance of any sort of possession, no matter how good something might be. Certainly it is good for us to be affirmed. But if I begin to crave that affirming and think that I can't go on in my service without it, I have made that experience an idol in my life to displace God. My affirmation needs to come primarily from Him, although you and I both know the frustration of His affirmation's seeming too abstract. I realize that I'm never going to get over that problem. I must stand on my guard always lest I slip into coveting what won't really satisfy my needs. How many hugs will it take till I am assured each time that my work has been good? How many reassurances do I need, to feel good about myself?

In contrast to the aching that can't be stilled is the wholeness that I felt last Thursday when I knew from the very depths of my being that I was doing what God wanted me to do. As I taught my classes and studied for some future teaching and worked on the writing of this book, I experienced a glorious day of freedom. I felt centered on God's will for my life and lived that day more fully aware of my calling. I kept thanking God all day long for the ecstasy I was experiencing, for, surely, that Joy was given to me as a particular treasure of His grace.

I don't always feel that way about my life and work. But I describe that experience for you (and for myself because at times I forget) to assure us that such moments are possible in our faith lives. There do come times for each of us when we can even feel the fact of our place in God's plans. I don't like to rely on such feelings, however, because they are not reliable. When we do experience them, though, we can note them in our memory to encourage us in the times when we doubt the action of God in our lives. He taught His people to build memorials to help them remember His faithfulness.

Surely, He is faithful! He has called us uniquely (each one of us) and given us gifts (for each of us His specially chosen combination) and personalities (with our own particular proportion of the fruit of the Spirit). We need always to be on our guard against those forces that would lead us away from our calling and into covetousness. Martin Luther called those forces "the devil, the world, and our flesh"; they are all the supernatural, human, and personal forces that lead us to greed.

Life does consist in our relationship with God, worked out in the actualities of daily situations. His desire is for us to know life and have it abundantly and eternally. All kinds of greed will steal that abundance from us and could even rob us of our desire for eternity. The question of the nature of the abundance will be discussed in future chapters of this book. At this point we know for sure that it cannot be obtained by coveting.

So much the opposite is true. Whenever we try to possess anything—objects or attitudes or people—the Joy of that thing will vanish, the freedom of the attitudes will be curtailed, the love of our relationships will be revealed as selfishness.

Let us be on our guard against such destruction. Then our lives can be filled with good stewardship of possessions, attitudes, and relationships.

Questions for Personal Application

1. What kinds of covetousness particularly afflict my life?

2. What was the proper role of Jesus in His earthly ministry?

3. What kinds of suffering does my calling entail?

4. How have I tried to grasp authority inappropriate to my calling?

5. How do I know what the will of God is for my life? What sorts of experiences have helped me find it?

6. At what times (perhaps right now) have I struggled to find the will of God? What sorts of things have helped me to find it more clearly then?

7. Can I ever completely settle the question of knowing God's will for my life? If not, how can I live with the tension that not knowing entails?

6 Hearing a Parable about Priorities

"And he told them this parable: 'The ground of a certain rich man produced a good crop. He thought to himself, "What shall I do? I have no place to store my crops."

" 'Then he said, "This is what I'll do. I will tear down my barns and build bigger ones, and there I will store all my grain and my goods. And I'll say to myself, 'You have plenty of good things laid up for many years. Take life easy; eat, drink and be merry.' "

" 'But God said to him, "You fool! This very night your life will be demanded from you. Then who will get what you have prepared for yourself?"

" 'This is how it will be with anyone who stores up things for himself but is not rich toward God.' "

—Luke 12:16-21

Once there was a beautiful ballerina. She wore the prettiest of gowns and danced the loveliest of ballets. She thought to herself one day, *I'm such a wonderful ballerina. How can I preserve my creative art for myself?*

So she hired a camera crew with the very best of equipment. She rented a magnificent hall with the latest in lighting and sound techniques. She contracted with the finest symphony orchestra and chose the most exquisite of classical ballet scores. She was so busy preparing things for her great production that she did not have any time to practice.

Finally, the big day came. Mechanically she went through the routines and didn't seem to notice that she couldn't perform very well at all. She made many mistakes and forgot certain sequences and missed her cues and the timing. Then she pushed the developers to prepare her films as quickly as possible, and, when they were completed, she set up her projection equipment and retired to a room by herself to admire her own creative art.

How distressing to realize that all the joy had gone out of the dance!

What do you think is the point of that story, my feeble attempt to write a parable? Trying to create one made me realize anew how good a storyteller Jesus was. Anyway, we could ruin the story by allegorizing it—by trying to match up each little detail of the story with a corresponding detail in the world of reality. We could try to figure out what the orchestra and the concert hall and the gowns and the sound equipment all stand for.

But that is the way to spoil a story. The artistry of a parable is that, unless otherwise specified (as in the case of the parable of the sower, in which Jesus defines the particular meanings for each of the elements), each detail is of value only in that it contributes to creating a whole texture from which we can see the great impact of the thrust of the story. My parable of the ballerina is intended to point out the idiocy of her attempt to save her gift for herself. The joy of her ballet was lost when she failed to share it with others.

Theologians call the one matching point between the parable and reality the *tertium comparationis,* or the third point of comparison. All the details of reality compose a very intricate web of conflicting ideas, emotions, purposes, meanings, and so forth. In the midst of it all, a particular quality can be more clearly understood by the creation of a story that illustrates that one point, that one bit of the reality of life. All the details of the parable weave a texture in which the main point is set out obviously.

If we want to read a parable properly, then, we want to notice each of the details, not to allegorize them, but to see how each contributes to the texture of the whole and how the main point can then be derived from the fabric laid out before us.

To understand a parable thoroughly, we must also notice carefully its context. Into what sort of situation was Jesus

The difference between an allegory (the story of the sower) and a parable can be illustrated like this:

Allegory

Story Details	Reality
seed	Word
path	devil steals
rock	no root
thorns	pleasures
good soil	faithful
crop	Christian life

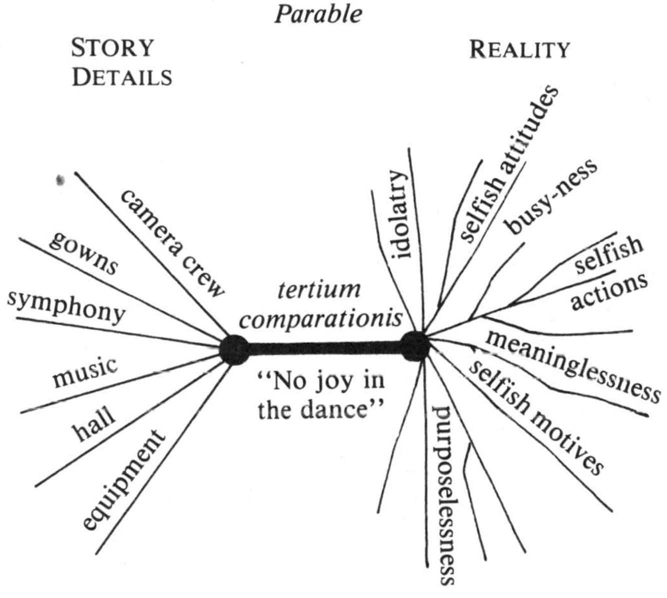

speaking? Who was His audience? How did they react? What sorts of introductory phrases does He use? And how does He end the parable? Does He leave His listeners hanging, or is there a punch line?

I ask my classes if parables are used by Jesus to make things clearer or to confuse His listeners. What would you say? You are right whichever answer you gave. Jesus used parables because they did make things clearer to those who were truly listening. To the ones who wanted to know the secrets of the Kingdom of God, the parables communicated deep truth. But many of the scoffers who came to hear Jesus probably dismissed His words as idle tales, not very profound, certainly not befitting a teacher who was supposed to bear so much authority. The truth was, in that case, hidden from their eyes so that, seeing, they did not understand.

For someone eager to learn the meaning of the Kingdom, however, the parables were excellent tools of instruction. They forced their listeners to mull them over in their heads; they encouraged continued reflection upon the words of Jesus. And in that further reflection, no doubt, the careful hearer would discover great insight.

Jesus was a brilliant teacher. He made His lessons just tough enough that they could not be taken for granted. They were simple enough to be appealing and couched in images that were homey and well known and made a lot of sense. He used everyday pictures to proclaim profound messages.

If we are reading a parable accurately, we should be both alienated and drawn by its main thrust. It should indict us—because most of the parables are about the Kingdom of God, and we have not yet reached any sort of perfection in it. And it should woo us—because deep inside our very innermost beings we all long for the Kingdom of God to become more of a reality in our lives.

Let us look carefully, then, at the texture Jesus creates

for us in this parable, and thereby be enabled to understand the point He wants to thrust home. We need to imagine ourselves in the place of the man who had asked Him to decide the inheritance, for this parable was told by Jesus in response to that request.

That context makes the first verse of the story very significant. Jesus says, literally, "A certain man being rich, the land brought forth plentifully." The description of the man is a participle, subordinate to the main verb which describes the action of the land. The man was rich, yes, but it was because the land brought forth plentifully. Right away this truth is set: the man's wealth is not the main thrust, but it is derived from the fact that his land produced abundantly.

Then, beginning with verse 17 and continuing through verse 19, we see the great self-centeredness and self-aggrandizement of the rich man. Notice this literally translated sequence of phrases:

> he was considering *in himself*
> what shall *I* do?
> for *I* do not have
> where *I* shall gather
> *my* fruits
> This *I* shall do
> *I* will tear down
> *my* storehouses and will build greater
> and *I* will gather there
> all the wheat and *my* good things
> and *I* will say
> to *my* soul-life
> *Self,*
> *you* have much goods being in store for many years
> rest *yourself;* eat, drink, be continually gladdened.

Obnoxious, isn't it? The texture that Jesus weaves is of a person totally centered on himself: patting himself on the back for his land's great productivity, wondering like the ballerina how he could more thoroughly hold to himself his own pleasure, trying to figure out the best ways to hoard his wealth.

Dwell on that texture with me for a little while so that you can catch the flavor of it penetratingly. The man begins by considering in himself. Catch sight of his smugness, stewing and planning and hoarding, all wrapped up into himself. He asks himself, "What shall I do? How can I make things work out even better for myself? How can I get all that is coming to me?" Yet all those things were his because he was graced to have land that produced plentifully.

But he doesn't remember that. Instead he complains, "For I do not have the place to gather all my fruits," and, of course, he thinks he deserves to have such a place since he is the one who possesses so much.

"Aha! Here is a plan; this is what I shall do. Aren't I wonderful that I should have such a brilliant idea of what I shall accomplish to solve my problem of storage? I will tear down my storehouses and build greater ones. Since my possessions are so magnificent, I should have more magnificent storehouses in which to preserve them. Then, I can gather into them all my good things. I can pile them up and watch the piles grow. And as I watch this fantastic accumulation of all my things, I will be able to say to myself, 'Self, you surely are wonderful that you have done such a good job of accumulating so much stuff. In fact, self, since you have so many goods in store for so many years, why don't you rest yourself now? It is time to enjoy all these terrific things that you have been working so hard to gather. After all, you had to do a lot of work to tear down your insufficient barns and build bigger ones. And there was so much you did to gather all your things into these larger barns. Now you deserve a break. Take it easy and rest yourself. Have a good time. Eat, drink, satisfy your own cravings. Feed your appetites and gluttony. Enjoy what you have, for you have plenty. Be continually cheered, for you have enough to go on a permanent binge.' "

Gross, isn't it? We can't help but cringe when we hear this picture in the words of Jesus. It is very easy for us to reject the rich man of the parable and yet fail to see how much like him we are ourselves.

That is the point of the parable. We must see ourselves in it and realize that our own self-centeredness, whatever forms it might take, is just as obnoxious. Lest we get overwhelmed by the fact of our sinful misfocus, however, we should finish looking at the text of this parable.

God speaks now against the self-centeredness of the rich man. "Foolish one," He says in the story of Jesus, "this very night they are requiring your soul-life from you. And what you have prepared, to whom shall it belong?" The noun which I have translated "soul-life" is the Greek word *psychos,* from which we get the term *psychology*. It means man in his totality, that very life principle which gives him his personal identity, the source of personality and the true essence of an individual, the basic principle of being that transcends and outlasts the mere biological lifespan of the body.

The verb in verse 20 literally means "they require" and is a common construction among Jewish rabbis to describe the action of God. It is God that requires this rich man's psyche. God is demanding the return. Much as in other parables, such as that of the man who gave his servants sums of money to be stewards of in his absence, so now God demands the reckoning. He calls this rich man to account for his stewardship.

I was in a play in high school called "You Can't Take It With You." I've often thought of that title in connection with this parable since then. When God asks the rich man, concerning all those things that he had prepared for his future, to whom shall they now belong, we wonder, too, now that his soul is being demanded of him. What is the sense of his having stored up all those goods when now it is revealed that he will not be able to make use of them?

We could do violence to the parable by saying at this point that it teaches us not to prepare for the future. That would be to miss the impact of its *tertium comparationis.* We must listen to the parable as it draws its own conclusion.

For now comes the punch line of the story, the sentence that tells us the point of the whole fabric. Jesus concludes, "Thus (for) the one storing up to himself and not rich to God" (verse 21, author's translation). The epigrammatic terseness of His conclusion makes the point stand out with greater starkness. Thus it is. There can be no denying this truth: life will prove to be vanity of all vanities if it is spent gathering goods that can't even be used. In the light of the fact that God requires the rendering of the soul, we must hear the call to avoid storing up to ourselves and choose instead to be rich toward God.

This parable of the rich man has some similarity to the parable of the rich man and poor Lazarus (Luke 16:19-31). This rich man, too, has had no concern for his needy neighbors or for God. But we must be wary of bringing the point of the Lazarus parable to this one and changing its emphasis. We dare not allegorize this one and match up the fields or the crops or the barns with certain objects in our experience. Similarly, we dare not moralize this story and teach it to our Sunday school classes with this conclusion: "Therefore, children, we can see that this man ought to have fed the poor." When we do such horrible moralizing of our gospel stories, we take the good news right out of them.

To moralize or to allegorize is to violate the parable. Jesus does talk about caring for the poor and about the responsibilities of our own stewardship, but not in this text. We will consider those implications more thoroughly in the context of passages that deal specifically with such conclusions. Here we must simply note the textures of the story and see its point of comparison with reality.

We have been overwhelmed with the story's fabric. We have reacted with discomfort to the I, I, I, I of this rich man's perspectives. Jesus, therefore, comes to this conclusion: "This is how it will be with anyone who stores up things for himself but is not rich toward God."

Now we can stress the point of the parable. It is not to sell our possessions and give to the poor. (That will be dealt with in chapter 9 of this book.) This chapter's point is simply this: get your priorities straight. Life consists in being rich toward God. It does not matter how much we can accumulate; it will not satisfy. Nor will we have the capacity really to enjoy it.

That takes us back to the man who had initiated this whole discussion with Jesus. Remember that he asked Jesus to serve as a rabbi in deciding for him a matter of inheritance. Jesus has told this parable to say, "Don't seek for the worldly goods of inheritance. Realize instead that life consists in being rich toward God."

Against all covetousness Jesus had warned him. "Keep watching," He had urged him. "Consistently be on your guard against the destructive effects of all kinds of greed."

So now the parable must speak to us. In connection with the previous chapter, we have already thought about all the kinds of greed and covetousness that afflict us. Now we must take that consideration one step further and think about the basic questions of our priorities. Is our life consisting in being rich toward God? Further chapters in this book will deal with some other practical applications of the priority question. At this point we probably should ask ourselves if we genuinely want God's priorities to be ours.

The man in the parable was called "foolish one." The real stupidity of his life was in his failure to realize that his own future was not in his own control. Because everything was "I," he mistakenly assumed that he could take care of his own future, too.

Similarly, often we think that we can control our destinies. We don't remember that there are a whole lot of other forces beyond our control.

Everyone has to have some sort of god. Either he will be storing up for himself, or he will be committed to some god outside himself. We need to weigh the gods to which our lives are committed. Are they worth our commitment, or will they turn to dust in our hands? Are the purposes for which we invest our time and energy and financial resources and creative abilities and thought worth that investment? What sort of criteria do we use to assess our commitments?

As I have thought about those questions, I have recognized that a particular outreach in my life is not a good investment. It is only a part of a part, I think to myself, to try to weasel out of confronting what I don't want to face. But God's grace can set us free enough to look at our uglinesses and be changed. I have to admit that in certain dimensions of a particular friendship I am being manipulative. The hidden motive is this attempt to store up for myself, to meet my needs instead of being real with the friend. And it is destructive to my relationship with God because I have made a god out of having my needs met. Seems like a petty matter, perhaps, but I realize painfully as I write this chapter that it is a clear case of misplaced priorities. And so it must be expunged. I want to clear out that which prevents me from being rich toward God.

I pray for you as you question some of the priorities of your life. I am sure that you don't have them all straight. None of us is yet able to be perfect. We must, therefore, be always on our guard against all kinds of covetousness. Life does not consist in storing up to ourselves, but in being rich toward God.

Questions for Personal Application

1. What misreadings of various parables have caused me to misunderstand God's Word to me? How can I learn better to read them?

2. What is the point of this parable about the rich fool?

3. How does that point apply to my life and priorities?

4. What are the major priorities in my life?

5. How have I misplaced some of my priorities, and what do I want to do about that?

6. How can I be set free from the kinds of fears that cause me to get my priorities out of line?

7. What happens when my relationship with God is more often chosen as the top priority of my life?

7 Seven Reasons Not to Worry

"Then Jesus said to his disciples: 'Therefore I tell you, do not worry about your life, what you will eat; or about your body, what you will wear. Life is more than food, and the body more than clothes. Consider the ravens: They do not sow or reap, they have no storeroom or barn; yet God feeds them. And how much more valuable you are than birds! Who of you by worrying can add a single hour to his life? Since you cannot do this very little thing, why do you worry about the rest?

" 'Consider how the lilies grow. They do not labor or spin. Yet I tell you, not even Solomon in all his splendor was dressed like one of these. If that is how God clothes the grass of the field, which is here today, and tomorrow is thrown into the fire, how much more will he clothe you, O you of little faith! And do not set your heart on what you will eat or drink; do not worry about it. For the pagan world runs after all such things, and your Father knows that you need them. But seek his kingdom, and these things will be given to you as well.' "

—Luke 12:22-31

One of my best friends is presently unemployed. He is retired from the military and a very gifted man, but the unemployment situation in Olympia is very difficult. Bill has tried his best to secure a job, and he has looked into all sorts of opportunities. The fact that he can't find work is not at all because of any laziness. He's getting very discouraged, as nothing turns up in spite of all his running.

Just before I sat down to start writing this chapter, his wife called me. He had been told by a friend that if he went to Idaho he could file for unemployment compensation there. (He is not able to do that in Washington because he receives a pension as a retired military officer.) Lydia called me to ask for my prayers because she didn't feel right about her husband's doing that.

It would be easy to write this chapter and say to you, reader, "Now don't ever worry. After all, God will provide for your every need." But I can't do that when I've been watching one of my dearest friends get more and more discouraged as no work turns up in spite of all his efforts. Besides, this is the second time this year; Bill had held the position from which he was released for only five months because the building industry is just too slow. The company that had hired him didn't have the financial stability to keep him on the payroll, even though he did excellent work for them.

So now what? How does a Christian react in such a situation? What does this passage from the mouth of Jesus say to the practical, nitty-gritty actualities of daily life in a world that is messed up economically, politically, and spiritually? Once again I can't be glib or give superficial answers. My friends are hurting, and that makes me hurt, too. I wish I had the money to give them to tide them over, but as a free-lance speaker I don't have such resources. Perhaps the best gift I can give them is to write this chapter as well as I can.

It is important for us to note in beginning that Jesus speaks these exhortations to His disciples. His words about not worrying would have no meaning for those not in a relationship with Him. Those who have to depend upon themselves for their needs have every reason to worry because there are a lot of circumstances outside their own control. But to the ones who are following after Him, Jesus gives seven reasons why they should not be worrying. One reason would be enough since it comes from Jesus, and His Word is sure. But He gives us the perfect number of reasons. (Seven is the biblical number symbolizing completion.) Everything we need to know to avoid the sin of worry is given in this list.

Jesus begins His list of reasons with the opening phrase, "Therefore, I tell you." That introduction tells us two very important things. First, it links us to the previous statement, considered in the last chapter of this book, that those who are storing up for themselves and are not rich toward God miss out on the real meaning of their existence. Because it is vanity to store up for ourselves, Jesus now goes on to tell us the opposite side. Not only should we not worry about having a big pile, but also we should not even worry about having the basics. Disciples do not need to live in a state of anxiety. If we seek the Kingdom of God, as this section concludes, everything else will fall into its proper place.

Second, the opening words of Jesus offer a deep assurance. He stresses, "I tell you." I can encourage my friends Bill and Lydia not to worry, but my words don't really carry any weight at all since I don't have the financial resources to back them up. But when Jesus says, "I tell you," we know that all heaven is at His disposal. We do not need to worry because He has *always* kept His promises. He has *always* provided for His people. He has *always* been faithful.

On the basis of His character, then, we hear the first reason. The Greek says literally, "Do not have anxiety to your soul-life [*psychos* again] what you might eat nor to your body, what you might clothe yourself with. For the psyche is more than the food and the body than the garment" (vv. 22-23, author's translation). The Jews to whom Jesus was speaking knew that God had created the body and that He had given it life. If He took care of those things, surely He would take care of the littler things—the food needed to sustain that life and the clothes needed to cover that body.

Jesus is arguing from the greater to the lesser. If the greater is true—if God is able to accomplish that—then surely the lesser will also be true. Paul uses a similar style of argument in Romans 8:32 when he writes, "He who did not spare his own Son, but gave him up for us all—how will he not also, along with him, graciously give us all things?" In other words, if God went so far as to give for us His very own beloved Son, won't He also give us everything else that might be necessary, but much smaller in comparison?

Certainly we do not need to have anxiety over the particulars of our lives when God has been so gracious to give us life. Our hearts and lungs work, we breathe, our blood circulates, and our bodies digest the food that He gives. Jesus invites us in this reason to be more concerned about the whole of life and not worried about the things that maintain it.

For the second reason not to worry Jesus invites us to "consider the ravens: They do not sow or reap, they have no storeroom or barn; yet God feeds them. And how much more valuable you are than birds!" (v. 24). It is significant that Jesus chose a bird that was unclean to Jewish people. And now He argues from the lesser to the greater. If God takes care of mere birds—and unclean ones at that—certainly He will take care of human beings who are far more valuable.

These verses have been used falsely by some as an encouragement to idleness or lack of planning. After all, the ravens don't gather into storerooms or barns, so why should we be careful about preparing? Such a misuse of Scripture points out the dangers of extremes in interpretation that arise from taking things out of context.

More and more I see that the Scriptures lay out for us a precarious balance between two extremes. That kind of balance was well illustrated by two members of our student house when I was in campus ministry. Jeff was a free spirit; he never planned for anything. He liked to "wing" things, and often wonderful surprises happened because he was so spontaneous and creative. Susan, on the other hand, was over-planned. She never did anything unless it was well thought out. The result was that she was extremely well-organized and did excellent work at whatever she planned. But she had a hard time enjoying anything that was spur-of-the-moment in its conception or initiation.

The two worked together as counselors for the youth group of a local church. And the combination of their two personality styles caused a lot of friction (which was humorous to those of us who listened to their mealtime confrontations), but it also caused a nice balance in the things that they did. Susan would work out details very carefully so that things would go smoothly. Jeff would bring in creativity and zest and spontaneity. Together they held each other's personalities in a creative tension that didn't fall into either extreme.

Sometimes they would joke together at mealtime. Susan would say, "You've got to plan ahead," and Jeff would answer back with a quotation from this passage about not worrying. But he knew deep inside that he needed Susan's planning, and he was grateful that she kept things from being done haphazardly.

Jesus does not speak against careful planning in this illustration; he speaks against worried planning. The key is in the phrase that runs throughout the section, "Do not have anxiety."

The third reason is this argument by negation: "It doesn't do you any good anyway, so why worry?" Jesus seems to ask. "Who of you by worrying can add a single hour to his life? Since you cannot do this very little thing, why do you worry about the rest?" (v. 25).

There is some confusion about the text of this passage. The word translated "single hour" could also be rendered "cubit." The word translated "life" could mean "height." Either translation is a good possibility. And both provide funny pictures to caution us against worry.

If the phrase should say, "Who of you by worrying can add a single cubit to his stature," the image is the ridiculous picture of someone trying to grow himself eighteen inches by stewing about it. Imagine a short Jewish man, four feet six inches tall, trying to be as tall as a Roman soldier of six feet. How could worrying accomplish such a thing? The picture is as ridiculous as putting a lamp under a bed instead of on a stand or of trying to hide a city set on a hill. Jesus uses absurd pictures to poke fun at the stupidity of some of our actions. Here we can't miss the point. It is just as ridiculous to imagine that by worrying about it we could grow ourselves.

We all know that a lot of genetic factors are involved in growth. There is not much we can do about our height. And who would ever think that such an enormous amount as a cubit, the distance from the tip of one's finger to one's elbow, could be added by the wasteful process of worrying?

If the text should be interpreted with the other option, the point is even more forceful. Who by worrying can add time to his span of life? We all know that the opposite is true. Probably the major reason for so many deaths by heart attack in our times is that we live in such an age of anxiety and stress. So many other diseases, like high blood pressure and so forth, are also caused by the terrible worry of our days. No, rather, the opposite will take place. We will take years off our life by worry. Isn't worrying a terribly foolish thing to do, then?

The irony of Jesus' comment is underscored by His conclusion. "Since you cannot do this very little thing," He jokes, and it almost seems like He is poking us in the ribs. Such a little thing: to add 18 inches onto our height or years on to our life span. "But if you can't do it," His humor presses us, "why do you worry about everything else?"

In other words, if we focused all our attention on one item of worry—in this case, adding inches or years—we would still not be able to accomplish it. Why, then, are we so involved in worrying about so many things? Worry can in no way be productive.

So far we have had an argument from the greater to the lesser, one from the lesser to the greater, and one from the ineffectiveness of worry. Now Jesus returns to the lesser and uses the flowers of the field. We are reminded of the passage about grass and flowers withering and fading in Isaiah 40 (see chapters 6 to 8 of my first book, *To Walk and Not Faint*).

We cannot be sure what flowers Jesus is referring to. Some commentators suggest the scarlet anemone on the basis of the use of the same word in the Septuagint text of Canticles 5:13, which speaks of the color of someone's lips. Other scholars nominate the autumn crocus, various types of lilies, the iris, or the gladiolus. It doesn't really matter. Wildflowers are all so beautiful, it seems. And they are indeed "God's extravagant hobby." He makes so many of them that last for such a short time, and in most instances nobody sees them except Himself.

The flowers don't worry about making themselves beautiful. They do not labor or spin. They do not stand there telling themselves to become beautiful. (Have you ever gone past a flower bed and heard the flowers grunting and groaning, "Come on. Get beautiful. Make colors"?) Yet, Jesus asserts, with all the forcefulness of His "I tell you" authority, "not even Solomon in all his splendor was dressed like one of these" (v. 27).

If God is so careful to provide everything for those flowers that soon will fade or be used as fuel for someone's fire, how much more will He take care to be sure that His people have the clothing they need? Jesus drives the point home a little more forcefully by adding, "O you of little faith!"

We must pay attention to that title. He means by that this blatant fact: that our worry actually comes from unbelief. We seem to think that food and clothing are ours because of our wonderful work—just like the rich man whose fields produced well and yet he patted himself on the back for their productivity. Just who do we think we are? Do we think that anything we possess has become ours by our own efforts and resources?

When I think that by my own toiling and spinning and worrying I can provide for myself, I get into the doubleminded unbelief against which James warns (see James 1:6-8 and 4:8). One side of us says that God is our Creator and Provider, and the other side of us takes that responsibility onto ourselves. How such unbelief must grieve our gracious heavenly Father!

I've learned recently what a slap in the face our worry is to Him. The lesson was hard to learn because my pride kept getting in the way. I have been working as a free-lance speaker and retreat leader for Christians Equipped for Ministry (CEM) since August of 1979. All along, the CEM board has stressed that they are responsible for the financial situation of our corporation. And yet, as I have said in a previous chapter, I kept thinking that I had to be sure to get enough speaking engagements to bring in enough money to pay my salary and our business expenses. Then this fall, when we added another staff person to be director of the ministry in our house community, I got uptight about how to bring in enough money to pay two salaries (even though we try to keep them low out of concern for living simply and world stewardship) . The CEM board kept telling me that the finances were not my problem. And yet I kept getting more and more worried about having sufficient speaking engagements that would pay enough.

Finally the board got it through my thick head. They put in my new letter of call the declaration that my salary was in no way dependent upon the honorariums that I receive. And they emphasized that my part of our covenant is to teach as well as I can (and my effectiveness gets obstructed for sure if I have to worry about making enough money) while their part of the covenant is to handle the administration and finances. I'm glad that I finally understand.

But I'm grieved that for so long I hurt their feelings. I didn't trust them with their part of the bargain. They had committed themselves to our ministry, and I didn't believe them for their faithfulness. I didn't trust them to take care of things adequately. My pride kept imagining that it was my responsibility to make it on my own. They kept asking me why I needed a board if I was going to insist on doing everything myself.

Why do we keep insisting that we provide for ourselves by ourselves? Our Father's responsibility is to provide for us. That does not mean, of course, that we don't work or try to get jobs or be careful to be good stewards of the financial resources we have.

The key is faithfulness. If we are faithful in doing the best we can with what we have—in time, gifts, abilities, finances, and so forth—we can confidently place ourselves into God's hands. His is the responsibility to clothe us, much more beautifully than He clothes the lilies of the field. He will clothe us with a radiance that can come only from the peace that is ours from trusting Him.

Verse 29 reinforces that balance and introduces the next reason for not worrying. Jesus says, "And do not set your heart on what you will eat or drink; do not worry about it. For the pagan world runs after all such things." The Greek says literally, "Do not be in anxious suspense." That is not mere advice on the part of Jesus; it is a command: "Do not investigate what you might eat and what you might drink."

To worry is to miss what life is about, so Jesus commands us not to let ourselves fall into that trap. "To not be in anxious suspense" is different from the injunction of verses 22 and 26. It pictures a person being suspended between the sky and the earth. Such a person doesn't have his feet firmly on the ground; he has no basis for security. Those who do not have knowledge of God will find themselves in such a state of suspension.

But for the disciple it should be different. We know who is the basis for trust and hope. Jesus' words are a subtle rebuke—"For those things all the nations of the world are striving." We are not to be like the pagans. They might have to be in anxious suspense about food and drink, but we who are the Lord's have the confidence of knowing Him and His provision for our needs.

When I was a sophomore in high school I got a mild case of measles, from which I at first seemed rapidly to recover. But I never really recuperated. As the weeks went on, I got weaker and weaker, more and more skinny and tired. I didn't know it, but the measles virus had caused my pancreas to malfunction, and I had become a diabetic.

For the few months before my diabetes was discovered, all I could think about was eating and drinking. I was ravenously hungry all the time, but could never gain any weight. At 5 ′6″ I got down to 84 pounds even though I was eating constantly. I'd sit in classes at school and plan what to eat or how I could get to the drinking fountain fast between classes. Constantly I ran to the fountain (and became a class joke because I drank too much), but none of us knew the reason for that terrible craving for water and food.

I remember the agony vividly—that terrible thirst that could never be quenched, that driving hunger that could never be satisfied. And I also remember the relief when I was finally diagnosed as a diabetic and put on insulin. At last I could study without being so insanely thirsty. At last I could relax about trying to gain weight (now I battle the opposite problem). The difference between before and after insulin was like going from a ravaging, blinding, terrifyingly hot desert without any wells to the lush green comfort of the Pacific Northwest forests.

Jesus wants the same kind of release for us all. One of the many reasons I have for gratitude in the midst of chronic disease is this realization that I have learned such good lessons from it about the provision of the Lord. We do not need to be in anxious suspense about how we will get enough to eat. The pagans have to worry so, because they don't know the intimate love and care of a heavenly Father.

That leads to this sixth reason that we do not have to worry: the positive reminder that our Father knows what we need. God is not stupid. He knows. He is not insensitive. He cares. He is not unable to provide. He is almighty. Why, then, do we doubt Him?

Jesus does not say that to blast us. He tells His disciples gently, to remind them that it is perfectly safe to place their entire lives and futures into the hands of the Father. After all, He knows specifically all the details of our needs, and as the psalmist reminds us, "Those who seek the Lord lack no good thing" (Psalm 34:10b).

I remember when I was first working in a parish and ran out of money. My job was an experiment. Just a few families in the congregation had banded together to pay me a minimal salary for initiating a campus ministry. Someone in the congregation lent me a car since I was not earning enough to pay for one, and members of the parish were helping me all the time to take care of my needs.

One day at the end of a month, however, I had absolutely no money left and needed some groceries. I was fretting about that when I went to church, but had not told anyone about my financial crunch. Later in the morning I went out to the mailbox to check for business. In the box was a small envelope with my name on it and nothing else. And inside was a $10 bill. I have no idea who put that there. But it was a sure sign that my heavenly Father knew I had need of things.

Later in that same year a former student of mine from my literature of the Bible class at the university shot a deer with his bow and arrow and gave me all the meat. We had not lacked for food that year, although we had eaten a lot of oatmeal and powdered milk and other such things that could be bought in bulk cheaply. And then God added that nice surprise of venison. Ha gave to the Israelites similarly, not only the manna of constant provision, but also the special gift of quail.

The last reason in the argument of Jesus is a positive drawing together of everything. "Seek his kingdom [instead of worrying], and these things will be given to you as well" (v. 31).

We know from other passages and accounts in the Scriptures that we cannot glibly say, "The Lord's people will have everything they need." Sometimes the righteous suffer. Check out the martyrs in the great faith chapter in Hebrews (chapter 11). Many of their situations did not turn out victoriously. But those who lost even their lives would not have changed the outcome for anything, I'm sure. They had truly learned the meaning of the promise in verse 31.

For those whose top priority is the Kingdom of God, nothing else matters. Even if a person has no physical security in this life, that uncertainty is not a cause for worry.

It is easy to write such a sentence and deathly hard to live it. I say deathly because it demands a death to ourselves to give up our efforts to secure our own futures and necessities. I had a very trying experience this summer groping to understand the meaning of this verse.

I had been led by God—at least, I had thought He was the One leading me—to buy that big five-bedroom house in order to provide a home for women suffering from emotional trauma and unable to survive alone. I knew the need. I felt compassion for their situations because of my own painful experience of rejection and depression. I believed that I was seeking the Kingdom in trying to initiate such a ministry.

But between the day of signing the agreement and the

final closing date, some of my financial resources failed to materialize, and I was $6000 short for the down payment. Since that amount was my entire salary for a year, there was no way I could raise the money myself or get any credit from a bank to borrow it. I had already borrowed every little bit I could from my parents and gathered all my savings, and I wasn't sure where else to turn.

I happened to be teaching in Alaska for the month of August and tried while I was up there to secure the needed finances, but nothing was working, and on Monday of my last week in Anchorage I was terribly discouraged. I asked the classes I was teaching for their prayers concerning this vision of the house ministry and the Christian community I wanted to establish. Perhaps I had misunderstood God's way of spreading the Kingdom through me. Or if I was right in seeking His Kingdom through such a ministry, I needed to trust better that He really was going to provide the finances that I needed in time.

I hoped that someone there might be able to lend me part or all of the $6000 I lacked. But nothing happened Monday. Nor Tuesday. Nor Wednesday.

Wednesday was my birthday. I didn't think that anybody knew it was my birthday, but my morning class surprised me with a party and gave me a brand-new suitcase to replace one that had gotten demolished at the airport. But no possibility for borrowing money came that day, so, in spite of the lovely birthday celebrations, I went to bed quite discouraged. I had just one day left in Anchorage; when I returned to Olympia I was expected to make the closing payment on the house. When I woke up on Thursday I cried, "God, this is Your last day!" Had I missed His purposes entirely? What was the meaning of that promise that if we are seeking His Kingdom everything will be added to us as well?

I knew that I was seeking His Kingdom. I had known His direction throughout all the planning. The CEM board believed in the vision, too. Many people had stressed the need, and many more were excited about this plan for ministry. But I was still short $6000 and had no idea of what I should do if I couldn't buy the house. Too many things had directed me toward that particular house—its location, its homeyness, its flexibility, its price and condition and so forth.

Thursday was indeed God's last day. At 9:00 A.M. a friend that I'd known back in Moscow offered to lend me $4000. At 10:00 A.M. the lady with whom I was staying offered to lend me $500. At 6 P.M. my father, whom I'd been trying to reach by phone for three days, told me that he'd sent to my bank $1000 more than I'd expected.

So with superecstasy at 9:30 P.M., after teaching my evening class, I called my CEM secretary to tell her that we would have the finances to make the house purchase. She then informed me that the board had decided to gather the money for me if I needed it because they believed in the vision too. So not only did I have $5500 of the $6000 I needed, but I also had their assurance that they thought, too, that the plan really was of God. I believed more deeply than ever that I had been following His guidance in seeking His Kingdom in such a way.

And then came the greatest surprise of all. I left the office of the Lutheran Church of Hope in Anchorage, Alaska (an appropriate name, I keep thinking), at 10:00 P.M. on August 21, 1980. The secretary met me at the door and handed me an envelope. "You should open this," she said, and I thought that was a strange beginning. "It was under my blotter, and it had your name on it so I opened it, thinking that it was part of the love offering for your ministry. But I sealed it right back up and put it under my blotter again so it was safe all day."

That was the strangest thing I'd ever heard. I felt awkward. There were several persons gathered in the hallway—all curious as to what was going on. I opened the envelope and could not believe my eyes. Inside was a note which said, "Have the happiest birthday ever," and it was signed, "Someone who loves you." And inside were ten $100 bills!

Oh, my God! How could I have doubted you? You have promised that if we are seeking the Kingdom "these things" will be given to us as well. Now I had more than enough for the down payment on the house and to recarpet the basement so that my bedroom and office could be put down there.

Now I sit in that basement and write this book and marvel at the grace of God. He will take care of the rest if we are seeking His Kingdom.

I have no idea who gave me that incredible birthday gift. It was God for sure.

However, as I have thought about this situation for the past four months, an even deeper awareness has grown in me. Even if God had not provided the $6000 I needed, He would still be God. Perhaps His answer to my needs might not have been to provide the money. Then we could have trusted Him that His purposes would be better fulfilled in other ways than through this EPHESUS house ministry.

You might be thinking, *Well, God doesn't do such spectacular things for me.* Perhaps it might not seem that way. He might be working in your life by giving you a well-paying job to provide for all your needs. Perhaps you are unemployed also now and share the grief and frustration of my friends whose story I told you at the beginning of this chapter. I am sure, however, that whatever your situation might be, this promise must apply. If you seek His Kingdom, other things will be yours as well. How that is worked out is specifically appropriate, in the infinite wisdom of God, for the particulars of our special situations.

One of my greatest frustrations with the church is that

we don't take this verse seriously. If we are concentrating on all the Kingdom of God involves, our behavior will be appropriate as the conduct of those who have chosen God's will and rule in their lives. Then we will not only trust God to provide for our needs, but we also will seek for better ways to make this verse come true in the lives of others.

For example, Bill's problem of deciding whether or not to go to Idaho to register for unemployment compensation bothers me for three reasons. First of all, even if the Washington law preventing his registering here is wrong, it is the law nonetheless. We do have a responsibility to uphold such laws even as we fight to change them. I believe that if we so seek the Kingdom, God honors our faithfulness in being true to the authorities over us.

Second, it seems to me that it would be double-mindedness to go. He has recently applied for several good possibilities in jobs. I hope that he can have the courage to wait for God's provision for his needs rather than take matters into his own hands and seek finances by means of a strategem that isn't unlawful, but is a side-stepping of a law.

Third, I think that we who are his Christian friends are responsible to provide for him and his family when he is out of work. We are told to share with the members of the household of faith (Gal. 6:2, 10). The early Christian church gives us the model; some even sold their possessions so that anyone in need could be provided for. Why aren't churches like that anymore? I long for our congregation to choose to care in this matter and be the church to Bill's family. It is our privilege to share our resources with them, even as they share their resources of skills and love and eagerness to serve with all of us.

If we were all seeking His Kingdom, such crises would not be so immobilizing. Just imagine what the world would be like if the church could institute caring policies to provide for the needy in ways that didn't destroy their dignity, in ways that didn't perpetuate social dilemmas?

What would happen if we would take seriously the seeking of His Kingdom? The promise associated with Jesus' exhortation is more than enough reason to give up on worrying. And there are all those other reasons, too. Have you given it up yet?

Questions for Personal Application

1. Which reason for not worrying is the most forceful for me? Why?

2. Why are the pictures of ravens and flowers such comforting assurances to us?

3. What other images might be more comforting to us in our times?

4. What does it mean to me to seek the Kingdom of God?

5. How can we go on believing if it appears that God is not providing for our needs?

6. How can we avoid glib, pat-on-the-back answers when trying to minister to those whose situations in life seem to be a sufficient cause for worry? How can we help such persons learn better to trust?

7. How can I learn to be more stable in my trust myself?

8 The Gift of the Kingdom

"Do not be afraid, little flock, for your Father has been pleased to give you the kingdom."

—*Luke 12:32*

I had prayed for the young troubled boy for a long time. He had been coming to me for counseling for some severe problems of self-esteem that had led to some foolish actions in rebellion against those who had hurt him. I listened to his confessions and cared about him in his grief, but I really longed to get him into the Scriptures so that he could learn God's principles for changing his life.

Then one day as we were driving on the freeway, he started telling me about some of his confusions about his faith. Suddenly, he looked at me and said, "What I would really like to do is study the Bible."

I responded, "Well, you know, don't you, that I give private Bible studies to people that are really interested in discipleship?"

"No, I didn't know that," he almost screamed. "Would you do that for me?"

Would I? Would I! I was so delighted I could hardly contain myself. Just what I had been wishing I could do for him, he now was asking me to give him. Our Bible studies together began within a week.

That little incident taught me some lovely lessons about the picture of the heavenly Father that is given us in this verse. Jesus says that the Father has been pleased to give us the Kingdom. The very thing that we were told to seek in the previous verse is now declared to be the Father's best will for us—in fact, His very pleasure to give us.

Verse 32 is so loaded with important concepts for our discipleship that we need a whole chapter to consider its few simple phrases. One little sentence speaks volumes of comfort and assurance and grace.

The verse is a very important link to the whole previous section. There Jesus gave us seven reasons why we do not need to worry; He concluded with the positive action we should be taking instead. If we are busy seeking first His Kingdom, we will not have any reason to worry about other things. They will be added to us as well.

Now He goes one step deeper and tells us that we do not need to fear. Fear seems to me to be the cause of most worry. I get afraid that my needs will not be met, so I worry about that or about how I will cope with it when they aren't. But if that fear can be taken away, I don't need to worry about anything. I can be confident that I will be able to handle it or that whatever it is that concerns me will indeed be worked out.

Once Jesus has commanded us to keep seeking the Kingdom, He immediately assures us that it has already been given so we don't need to fear that such seeking will be in vain. The Greek imperative we translate "seek" is in the present tense in verse 31. That means it is a continuous action of seeking that we are exhorted to be involved in. Similarly, the imperative translated "do not be afraid" in verse 32 is also in the present. We can continue not fearing all the while that we are seeking. Our search can always take place in great confidence. The two verbs work together even more tightly, furthermore, because when we are not afraid, we are set free all the more to seek.

One by one the fears that I had of entering a free-lance speaking ministry are passing away. The CEM board is finally convincing me of their love and support, and that is freeing me to enter into my work with greater conviction. I feel free to accept tougher jobs or to do things without financial remuneration or to spend as much time as I need to study in preparation for some event. More and more I'm finding myself filled with ecstasy because of the Joy of doing what I believe I'm called to do. The less fear I have, the more fun it is to seek the Kingdom. The more free I am, the less hesitation I have to let God change my directions.

I am all too human, however, so it has been hard for me to learn, and I have only begun. But that constant necessity for the process makes me want to reach out of the pages of this book and ask how you are doing with your seeking of the Kingdom and your fears. What sorts of things hinder you from a constant seeking of the Kingdom? What assurances are necessary for you to be able to lay aside your fears? How will the freedom from fear enable you more diligently to seek the Kingdom? What things still stand in your way?

Please take time to consider those questions now before you go on reading. Then we can be more open to hear the rest of the tremendous comfort of this verse from Luke 12.

As I paused with you to think of the reasons fear disrupts my search for the Kingdom, I realized that most of my fears arise from my terrible need for security. Jesus' next words minister to that need directly so it is exciting for me to go on with this study. Jesus now addresses His disciples as "little flock." This is the only place in the New Testament where that phrase occurs, so we are urged by its uniqueness to pay special attention to its connotations.

The idea of a flock is a theme that weaves throughout the Scriptures. For Jesus to use that term causes His Jewish hearers to remember all sorts of Old Testament images as well as statements that He has made during His ministry among them. A bit of tracing of that theme will reveal to us a name of immense comfort.

From the very beginning sheep were part of the sacrifices the people of God offered to Him. Consequently, certain sheep were set apart for special purposes. Flocks kept near Jerusalem were designated explicitly for use in the Temple offerings and were guarded wth great care so that they would not be spoiled. (It is a strong possibility that the flocks being guarded by the shepherds on the night of Christ's birth were so designated—which increases the significance of their shepherds' being chosen to be the first to go to worship the Lamb of God.)

In the time of the prophets the imagery of flocks and shepherd took on deeper significance. God had allowed the flock of Israel to be taken away into captivity (Jer. 13:17). The priests and leaders who should have been caring for them had failed in their job, and the people had turned away from the Lord. But God promised that someday He would send a shepherd who would properly care for the sheep, one who would rescue them and guard them and nourish them appropriately (Ezek. 34).

Between Leviticus, which describes the offerings of sheep, and Ezekiel are several lovely pictures of the grace of the Shepherd. Isaiah portrays the Lord coming to feed His flock like a shepherd (see my comments in chapter 11 of *To Walk and Not Faint*). And, of course, we all know the comforting picture in Psalm 23 of the Good Shepherd and His tender care for us, His flock.

Jesus applies all those Old Testament images of the care of the sheep to Himself when He calls Himself the Good Shepherd in John 10. In the intricate discourse of that chapter He tells us about His voice calling the sheep, and of His sacrificial death for them, and of the security of His care for them. No one is able to snatch the sheep out of His hand, He promises (John 10:28).

When He calls His disciples "little flock" here, then, the name breathes tenderness and infinite love. We see in that name His death for us and the security of being in His hand. And thereby we are encouraged not to fear.

Even the word *little* speaks to me an inverted sort of

comfort. The flock may be small; it may seem that the whole world is against us; we may not have much power according to the world's standards; yet we are the precious flock of God. We do not have to fear because of our size. If we are seeking the Kingdom, it will happen in our midst, and we will be part of its great power and effectiveness. It does not matter at all how little we might be.

We may be just stupid sheep. We for sure are weak and helpless in the face of danger. The number of true disciples, those committed to a constant search for the Kingdom, may be small indeed and naive in our innocence. But we have an infinitely caring Shepherd, One who deals with us tenderly and yet raises His mighty arm on our behalf (Isa. 40:10-11).

In newspapers produced by organizations doing ministry behind the Iron Curtain I have read several accounts of phenomenal experiences of the protection of God. Christians in those lands of oppression endure great hardship and tyranny, and yet they know the reality of the Shepherd's gentleness. They may be a little flock, but they are exerting a large influence among their neighbors. A few weeks ago, my housemate Julie read some excerpts from a book called *A Song in Siberia,* which describes the influence of those brave and courageous Christians. Even their Communist oppressors have to admit the power of their lives; they have truly learned the meaning of Christ's loving title in this verse.

The final phrase is probably much better understood by those who are parents than by me, although it was my privilege to experience its truth in the incident related at the beginning of this chapter. You know what a joy it is to give to your children that which you know is good for them, that which you had already decided you wanted to give them in the first place.

The verb tenses are again significant here. When Jesus says, "Your Father has been pleased" to give us the

Kingdom, the verb indicates a once-and-for-all past action. It was already decided. It is undoubtedly His will; there will be no hesitation whatsoever.

The infinitive "to give" is also an aorist verb, which means that it, too, is a decisive, completed action. Because the first verb is in the past tense, the whole phrase means that God has already decided and already bestowed upon us the gift of the Kingdom. In other words, as we keep searching for it, we shall undoubtedly keep finding it constantly, because it has already once and for all been given. That makes the search overwhelmingly rewarding.

Don't you like to search for something that you know for sure you will find? And how happy it must make the Father when we ask for something that He has already decided to give us—in fact, He has already given it!

I am fortunate to have a wonderful earthly father, so the fact that the One who has been pleased to give us the Kingdom is called Father is deeply meaningful for me. To me the name implies tender concern, great sacrifice, awesome love, infinite patience, willingness to take time, instruction in important things, chastisement in order to help me grow, provision for all my material needs, affirmation, and affection. My father was not perfect, of course, but our heavenly Father is. And in His perfection He has chosen to adopt us as His children, to make us His own, and, therefore, to lavish upon us all the gifts of His most abundant grace.

Specifically here those gifts are seen to flow from this prior decision: that He has been pleased to give us the Kingdom. Paul talks about that choice, made in fact before the foundations of the world, and about all that the Father's choice entails in his hymn of praise at the beginning of his letter to the Ephesians (1:3-14). The eternal, loving purposes of this gracious Father are too overwhelming ever to be thoroughly grasped. We cannot react except to fall on our knees in wonder and awe.

It remains for us to consider what the Kingdom is. We have already been given it, and we receive it as much as we keep seeking for it. What is it? The Kingdom must be defined, first of all, in terms of its King. For the Kingdom to happen, the King must be its Ruler. When we seek the Kingdom, then, we are asking for Christ to rule in our hearts and lives. We want Him to be the Master over every dimension of our existence.

If we want the Kingdom to be spread in the world, moreover, we will want to be involved in the process of extending its influence. We will want the characteristics of God's Kingdom to affect other dimensions of human existence. And Jesus Himself proclaimed at the beginning of His ministry what the Kingdom consisted of. When He returned to the synagogue of His home town, He announced to all His neighbors and friends what His ministry was going to be about. Then He prophesied that they were not going to like it, and they tried to throw Him over a cliff. A really scary scene—but it realistically shows us that the Kingdom Jesus initiated and uses us to initiate further into the world is not desired by everyone. In fact, many people are going to be downright hostile to it. So our seeking of the Kingdom will draw us into suffering for its sake.

The Joy of its extension in the world, however, will be well worth whatever suffering it might entail, for the following ministries will characterize the Kingdom, according to the prophet Isaiah, from whose scroll Jesus read on that greatly significant day in Nazareth. The One called to initiate the Kingdom was anointed by the Spirit and commissioned for these tasks:

> "To preach good news to the poor.
> . . . to proclaim freedom for the prisoners
> and recovery of sight for the blind,
> to release the oppressed,
> to proclaim the year of the Lord's favor."
>
> Luke 4:18-19

When Jesus had rolled up the scroll again and sat down to teach, He said, "Today this scripture is fulfilled in your hearing" (Luke 4:21). As we join Him in bringing the Kingdom to our broken world, we are commissioned for the same tasks.

I don't think I've barely begun to understand the significance of the fact that the Father has already been pleased to give us the Kingdom of Christ. It means for me personally security, and love, and acceptance. But it also means that if I am seeking to be a minsiter to others He will give me—no, He has already given me—everything I need to do that. That is so powerful I hardly know how to write about it.

If I want to set someone free from whatever prisons might have him shackled, for example, I already have the resources at my disposal to set him free. I can proclaim good news to the begging poor and release them from the oppression of their grinding poverty.

One of the best examples in our times is Mother Teresa. Truly she has grasped the power available in this verse. She and her sisters move out boldly into the streets of Calcutta bringing good news to the poor in the face of seemingly insurmountable obstacles. The world has recognized her power and the good she has brought and continues to bring by awarding her the Nobel Peace Prize in 1979. The radiance and Joy that she expresses could only be the result of a deep awareness that she is already the possessor of the Kingdom of God and of all she needs to bring that Kingdom to others. What a model she is to us!

As we keep remembering the assurance of this verse, we learn new lessons about the previous one. To realize how the Father has been pleased to give us the Kingdom enables us to seek it, trusting that everything else we need will be added to us. We are seeing that here in the EPHESUS Community in some exciting ways. The beginnings of this house were so miraculous that we just *know* that this is

God's house, set aside for His purposes. Sometimes I feel like tiptoeing around because I'm walking on holy ground.

Since we know, then, that the Father has been pleased to give the Kingdom to those in this place, we can grow into a greater confidence about whatever is necessary to carry on the ministry here. And I have seen time and time again how God has provided.

When I first wrote this chapter, I illustrated that last statement by telling how the Lord provided a house director for our ministry to persons needing a place to stay. Now tonight as I revise this chapter I'm realizing how wonderfully comforting it is to me to read these things again. Our house director has decided to return to her ministry of music, and earlier today I was worrying a bit about how God would have us go on with the work we have begun. As I caught myself fearing how we would find a new director, I reread what I had written about finding the first one. With a surge of Joy I remember that God is still in charge. He will again provide whatever we need for whatever directions He wants us to pursue. Our first director was His gift for the ministry that we could do while she was here. Now the form of that ministry might change, but the Kingdom that we are seeking to spread will not. We can trust, therefore, that its King will make sure that "these things" are added.

Time and time again I am amazed at the perfection of the Father's gifts for the Kingdom's work to be done. Just when we recognized that we needed firmer beds, a family in my church gave us a pair of twin beds. Just as our house began to fill up with extra guests, some women I'd met at a retreat sent us two extra blankets. Just at Christmas time when food was running low, a family chose to give, instead of gifts to each other, a box of groceries for us. We have much more than we need.

Now I'm eager to start learning to apply this awareness to some of the practical situations that have, in the past, given me great fear. For example, I'm frightened of things going wrong, partly because I can't see well enough to fix things and also because I have absolutely no mechanical ability. Remember my telling you of my discovery that one whole corner of my office floor was soaked? My friend Doug has come over several times to check the walls, to fix the leak in the bathroom upstairs, and so forth. But still the floor is soaked, despite all our efforts to dry it and to find the cause of the problem.

My first tendency is to be frustrated, panicky, worried about how things will be taken care of. Slowly I'm learning to believe that this inconvenience is no big deal. The Kingdom will happen in this house despite the mess. My books can be written and my lessons prepared in spite of the obstructions. And the Kingdom will happen more powerfully through me, the more I learn that if I keep seeking the Kingdom, even such things as the finding of the source of a wet floor will be added as well.

That illustration sounds foolish, I am sure. And I know that I am foolish in my mistrust of the Father. We are appropriately called sheep. Yet it has been His good pleasure to give us the Kingdom. I long to learn to trust Him in everything and to keep seeking the Kingdom without worry or fear about other little things that trouble my life. He cares for ravens and lilies. He provides me with food and raiment. Surely He can also (most likely through friends who are helping me) take care of a wet floor.

Meanwhile I am getting more and more excited about the privilege of serving Him in the ministry to which I am called in the Kingdom. And what about you?

Now it is very late at night. I'm feeling such a pleasant mellowness as I think about the privilege that is ours to belong to the Kingdom. Part of the Father's good pleasure is to strengthen us for the work of His Kingdom. I am eager to receive that strength in sleep and rest. It will be pleasant now to lie down and rest thinking about how the

Father has already given us the Kingdom. What need for fear? I am part of the beloved flock of Christ. He is the Good Shepherd, and His most favorite thing to do is care for us, His sheep.

Questions for Personal Application

1. What sorts of things do I fear?
2. Why do I fear those things?
3. How can the Good Shepherd deliver me from my fears?
4. What does the name, "little flock," mean to me?
5. What is my understanding of the term "Father"? What connotations does that bring?
6. How does it help me to know that He has already been pleased to give me the Kingdom?
7. What does it mean that we have been given the Kingdom?

9 To Care for the Poor

"Sell your possessions and give to the poor."
—Luke 12:33a

I asked how many of the persons whose bodies were scattered all along the streets of New Delhi were dead.

"About half of them," our guide answered. "And the rest will be dead by tomorrow." I watched the street workers come by with their huge wheelbarrows. They scooped up the bodies of those who were dead and threw them from their shovels into the carts to be taken to the city dump for burning. My whole insides felt like garbage.

Everywhere we went in India, we were met by hungry children, destitute and forlorn, some crippled (purposely maimed by their parents, I'd been told, in order to get more alms), all skinny and gaunt with glazed eyes. "Baksheesh," they cried again and again. I heard that pitiful cry in my sleep.

"You give me money; I dive off tower," the beggar wheedled.

You're kidding, I thought. *There is only a shallow few inches of water in that moat, and that tower is a hundred feet tall.* "You'll be killed for sure."

"It doesn't matter," our guide told me. "If he dies, he hopes to be reincarnated in a better life. Most people give him some money and tell him out of 'pity' that he doesn't need to dive." His was simply one of a hundred different tactics for begging.

About a month later I returned to the United States

from that choir tour around the world. I was aghast at all the swimming pools in people's yards when we flew into New York City. One of the first things I saw in the airport was an overly furred woman leading her dog on a gaudy, bejeweled leash. He was wearing a rhinestone collar and looked as if he had just had his hair done. I suffered an extraordinary culture shock that has not left me yet, more than ten years later.

I will never forget the faces of the poor. I will never forget the sound of their cries. I will never lose my shame. They are starving, and I have too much.

It is hard to write this chapter because I want desperately to communicate to you the intensity of what I am saying. I wish I could show you my slides from India and the Orient, but I'm sure that even that wouldn't really enable you to understand the pain. You need to be there—to hear the agonized cries, to smell the filth, to watch the beggars die, to know that you are too wealthy and too well-fed, to be overwhelmed with the shame of the failure of the church to believe and follow the words of Jesus.

"Sell your possessions," He keeps saying to us, "and give to the begging poor." We must learn what that sentence means in its context, because in it lies the secret of possessing the Kingdom of God.

I just called my housemates down to my writing office to pray with me before going on with this chapter. The subject is so important to me and such a great source of grief that I was afraid of the task of putting it down on paper. I teach about our responsibility to the poor often, but then I am face to face with people. I can read their reactions and soften my words accordingly. I am afraid of blasting so hard that you will stop reading this chapter, that you will get uncomfortable with my words and give up on this book. I want you to hear all the love underneath my words.

It is a terrible tragedy that we, the people of God, are not living according to the instructions of Jesus in verses such as this one. And I think that we hurt not only those who are consequently deprived of adequate food, but also ourselves. We are missing out on the fullness of the Kingdom because we have too much. This is the principle: we don't know how to feast because we don't know how to fast.

Please hear me carefully. Know that the Good News of forgiveness in Christ underlies my words, that the gospel message of God's acceptance of us in spite of our shame is beneath even my most potent blasts. But do listen to the indictments. For we are all individually as well as corporately guilty.

In Appendix A I have listed some of the better resources I have found in my concern for the poor of the world. There you will find names and addresses of organizations worthy of your support, titles of books that teach about the subject of world hunger much more effectively than I ever could, and texts from the Scriptures that are good for study. Please make use of those resources to follow up the message of this chapter.

If your consideration of this subject stops after you have read this chapter, I will have failed. I beg of you to hear this introduction and then take seriously what you can do about the subject in your own personal, family, church, and political life.

I think that the context of this verse is critically important. Jesus has just assured His disciples that the Father has already been pleased to give them the Kingdom, and that promise affects our understanding of His next immediate instruction. Not only does the prior possession of the Kingdom free us to do what He asks, but also He seems to be implying that we won't really possess the Kingdom unless we follow this instruction.

First of all, let us rejoice in the fact that we know we

have the Kingdom. We don't have to be afraid of being generous. When Paul instructs the Romans how to use their gifts, he says to exercise the gift of showing mercy with cheerfulness (Rom. 12:8). The Greek word there actually says "hilarity." "Be merciful with hilarity." Isn't that an exciting invitation? I think that far too often we miss out on the fun of giving because we don't show mercy with the kind of abandon and freedom the verse encourages.

The Father has given us the Kingdom; therefore, we can pour out our substance for the benefit of others and know that we can never outgive a gracious and generous heavenly Father. Paul says in his second letter to the Corinthians that the One who gives seed to the sower and bread to the eater will give us all that we need for our own existence plus extra so that we have plenty to give away (2 Cor. 9:10-11). We need to loosen up our inhibitions and realize that being generous is not only fun, but also the most fulfilling way to live.

Second, however, the context forces us to realize that we have not experienced the Kingdom as thoroughly as we could because we have not sold our possessions and given to the poor. We do not know how to feast—to enjoy the Kingdom—because we have not learned to fast. A small incident from the beginning of my professional ministry will illustrate the point.

When I first began working in campus ministry, my job was an experiment, so my salary was minimal—enough to get by, but only if I pinched my pennies carefully. I didn't really care how much money I had because I loved my work. It was my privilege to do all the things I really love to do—teach the Scriptures, direct choirs, train Sunday School teachers, and visit with students from Washington State and the University of Idaho. I was extraordinarily happy.

But it was necessary to live simply. I had guests often for

dinner, but they knew they would get food that was inexpensive and easy to prepare. They came for conversation and not any sort of gourmet fare.

I was happy. I didn't have to worry about entertaining with distinction, so I could be comfortable simply to serve an easy meal and concentrate on loving those who came.

You can imagine my delight, then, when two close friends coming to my apartment brought all the fixings for a steak dinner. That was a royal treat too good to believe, a highlight experience because it was an unusual feast. I still remember that gift distinctly because it was unique.

It was a real steak. And such a celebration! Now perhaps you don't get very excited about having steak for dinner, but it was a treasure to me—steaks and tomatoes, plump Idaho potatoes, and everything that goes with such a feast. It was a housewarming gift, and a spectacular one.

I am convinced that in our culture we do not know how to feast and celebrate because we do not know how to fast and abstain. Because most families can have special foods every night of the week, because there are always cookies in the cookie jar and meat and ice cream in the freezer, there is nothing that constitutes an outstanding celebration. So when we celebrate Thanksgiving, we just overload and eat too much of everything in order to make it a special feast.

I'm not at all opposed to feasting, but to doing it too often. I think that these words from Jesus in Luke 12 provide us with a way to learn again to celebrate.

How much could you cut off your grocery budget if you took out all junk foods (that would also be more healthy for your family), cut in half your consumption of red meat (and used such things as tofu or soybean protein instead), and eliminated extra snacks (which would probably put everybody's hearts and body frames in better shape)? You could send all the money you saved to some organization dedicated to the feeding of the poor.

I know, however, that we need to be careful in our almsgiving. It does not help the poor to dump on them our charity. We need to find ways that enable them to build economic stability, resources that will help them get jobs so that they can provide for themselves. In other words, our care for them must be so loving that it preserves their dignity even while it ministers to their need.

That is why I support such agencies as World Vision International. That organization is dedicated to a fine balance of caring for the destitute and equipping them to build their own lives. They also have a good balance between physical aid to needy countries and spiritual equipping through pastoral training and education for the children in their programs. The two children I sponsor write to me about their love for Jesus. World Vision guarantees that its children will learn about Jesus, and the school reports I receive tell me specifically how Yin Man and Jessy are getting Christian education.

Other fine Christian agencies listed in Appendix A can send extraordinary amounts of food and medicine to poverty-stricken countries because the goods have been donated already, and they need from us only the money for shipping.

All our contributions for the poor will be insufficient, however, if the world's economic systems and governmental policies are still basically unjust or impractical. That is why I urge everyone to participate in Bread for the World, a political Christian organization working to effect policies in U.S. governmental legislation that will be more favorable to the poor here and elsewhere in the world. Bread for the World also does an excellent job of keeping its members informed of political activities in which they can participate to bring justice for the poor and oppressed.

All these comments about specific things we can be involved in are insufficient, however, if we are not ready to be involved in caring for the needy of the world as the people of God *together*. To understand the importance of God's plan for needy people, we need to go back to our Old Testament roots.

I was shocked about five months ago when I was preparing a Bible study on stewardship and learned from Deuteronomy 14 what the tithes were used for in the worship of the people of Israel. Regular gifts brought by the people to the tabernacle were used for celebrations, for paying the professional workers, and for caring for the poor and needy, especially the widows and orphans and aliens. None of the basic tithe was used for the building or the worship accouterments. All those things were given as special offerings over and above the tithe.

Do you know any church that has those priorities? I can think of only one that begins to come close: the Church of the Saviour, in Washington, D. C. You can read about their stewardship in books such as *Call to Commitment; The New Community;* and *Journey Inward, Journey Outward,* all by Elizabeth O'Connor.

But that church is unique in this country. Most of our churches spend the greater portion of their money on their buildings and upkeep and remodeling and other such things.

Many other problems in our churches are related to this. I remember reading a letter to the editor in *Christianity Today* in which the writer objected to an article's suggestions that Christians ought to be faithful about paying for songbooks to get the music written by Christian songwriters. She said that music is for God's glory and ought to be free to His people. I thought, *Surely. When the church starts using its tithes to pay for Christian artists' survival so that they could be free from financial strain, then I'm sure they would be glad to offer their music freely to the people of God.*

Similarly, I am distressed that my housemate is still looking with great frustration for a full-time permanent job. She has extraordinary gifts in art, but does not have much time to use them because she must maintain a job to support herself. If the church used its tithes to pay professional workers as in the Old Testament, congregations could afford to have musicians, artists, youth workers, educators, ministers for single persons, and so forth on staff so that more persons would be equipped to use their gifts for spreading the Kingdom of God.

See how much is tied into this verse? The Father wants the Kingdom to be happening in all kinds of ways, but most of them are getting obstructed because we haven't got our stewardship into line.

But it is the poor that concern me the most. I have watched dying beggars on the streets in India. I have worked in the inner city of Chicago. I write to a man on death row. I try to give away as much as I can for the hungry. But my personal guilt and our corporate guilt are so large that the answer to the question of "What can I do?" is always, "More!"

Why is it that Christians pay such good attention to all the promises of God in His Word, but don't listen very well to the instructions Jesus gives about caring for the poor? James again reminds us, "Religion that God our Father accepts as pure and faultless is this: to look after orphans and widows in their distress and to keep oneself from being polluted by the world" (James 1:27). That instruction involves both journeys of the Christian life (to use Elizabeth O'Connor's terms): the journey inward in private devotional reading, study of the Scriptures, and prayer to keep ourselves from the world's pollution, and the journey outward to care for those in need. That is the balance necessary for finding the Kingdom, and the Father has already made it possible for us to be possessors.

We live in a culture that makes it difficult to follow these instructions from Jesus. In our world, material prosperity is a sign of success. To accumulate great possessions is to convince everyone of one's value. But the products of this sense of values have been tyranny, oppression, and social injustice in all kinds of forms.

We are called by this text to be different from the world, to reject its values and systems that perpetrate injustice. And in so doing we show our trust in the Father's provision for our needs and our belief that His values for the Kingdom are the most fulfilling for our existence.

Note that Jesus does not tell us to sell *all* our possessions. To do so and create a class of beggars in the church would not further the Kingdom according to God's plan. We would become a burden to our society rather than part of its deliverance. Jesus is not denouncing private ownership; He is revealing its abuse. It is not wrong to possess things; it is wrong to possess too many of them.

Each of us must ask this critical question: How much is enough? For each of us the answer will be different according to our circumstances of work, ministry, family, and so forth. But we must individually ask that question seriously and take specific steps to right the wrongs of our possessions. And I think I can boldly say that all of us possess too much.

I don't mean by this chapter just to make you feel terrible about the things you own. But I do want to propose this new criterion for judging whether or not you should possess something: Does it enable you better to be seeking the Kingdom of God and extending it to others?

To possess too many things often leads to a trust in them, and that prevents real trust in God. Having too many things sometimes makes us so busy taking care of them that we don't have time to be taking care of people. But some possessions are necessary for us to do ministry and to be involved in the calling for which God has especially chosen us.

I wrestled with the question of buying a stereo. It took me two years to realize that it was a good investment in my ministry. Not only do I study and write better with classical music in the background, but also I have been able to teach others to appreciate fine music. For example, I have frequently used the Pachelbel *Canon* described in an earlier chapter to teach others about the faithfulness of God. The stereo has brought to me deeper seeking of the Kingdom of God, and it has been a tool for me to extend that Kingdom to others. The same might or might not be true for you.

Similarly, after much wrestling and prayer, I have invested in a good typewriter. And I did decide to buy this house to have a place to which women can come to stay when they need a Christian community to surround them with love. But I decided not to buy a car. My Kingdom seeking happens better without one.

I must daily ask questions of stewardship. Is it the best way to be seeking the Kingdom to buy these groceries or that article of clothing or that book? I don't need to live an ascetic existence and survive on bread and water. God did not create such a wonderful variety of foods and colors and textures for our lives to be boring and to lack beauty. But I don't need to eat pineapple, for example, if I know that pineapple companies are contributing to malnutrition in the children of farmers in Latin America. Perhaps if enough of us refused to eat pineapple, it would force those companies to take steps to correct conditions that we know cause retardation in children.

I need to be constantly questioning the policies of my world in order to avoid as much as I can those agencies that perpetuate injustice and oppression of the poor.

I was teaching about this subject one day at a youth congress and a friend said, "But, Marva, I can't be concerned about the starving of the world. I have all I can do to care about the kids that are selling drugs on the street in front of my house." I was grateful for his reminder. God calls each of us uniquely. There are certain injustices that you can be fighting that I don't have the skills to handle. There are certain questions that you must address because of where you live or where you work or what kind of family you have.

I don't mind if you come up with different solutions after you have thought through these difficult questions of stewardship. But have you thought about it?

I keep asking that question, "Have you thought about it?" because I fear that most Christians just fall into the habits of the world and never ask whether or not such behavior is worthy of the Kingdom.

Have you thought about it with your family? Have you talked it over with your children? Are you teaching them to care about the poor and the needy? Have you discussed it with your local congregation? Can you agree with the way the money gathered in your church is spent? I don't know of many congregations that even tithe, much less use the tithes according to God's principles. Just think what could be done in our churches if we used its money for celebration, the professional workers, and the poor. Isn't that an exciting prospect?

Please don't let this chapter slip away from your consciousness after you have read it. We do not need to be overwhelmed by the immensity of the task. Yes, the care for the needy of the world is too big of a task. But God has not asked us to solve it by ourselves. Jesus simply says, "Sell your possessions and give to the poor." Take care of your own little corner of the world. And together with your family and your neighborhood and your church and me and other groups also concerned, we can change the world.

But for the sake of the poor, start somewhere! May I suggest that today you decide with your family on some specific step with which you will begin your deeper concern for the poor. Maybe you can have one meatless meal a week and send the money saved to some organization feeding the poor. Maybe you can sponsor a child through

World Vision. A teenager that I've taught in Bible study groups decided to give up snacks and use the money for the poor. She put on the wall of her room a World Vision poster that said in stark white letters at the top, "How do you feed four billion hungry people?" The rest of the poster was black, except for a small picture of a little child down in the corner and the caption, "One at a time."

"Sell your possessions," Jesus urges, "and give to the poor." Start with one at a time today. Then let it grow as you discover the Joy of seeking the Kingdom and the freedom of not having to possess so much.

Questions for Personal Application

1. What are my attitudes toward possessions?
2. How can I solve the problem of how much is enough?
3. What sort of criteria do I use to guide my decisions about whether to purchase something?
4. What specific actions does my family take already to share with the poor?
5. How do my children feel about becoming more concerned for the poor?
6. What kinds of family activities could increase our awareness of the needy of the world?
7. Do we feast too much in our family?
8. Do we fast enough?
9. How could I get my church more involved in concern

for the poor?

10. What step will I take today in response to Jesus' command in Luke 12:33?

11. What other sections of the Old Testament address the issue of the poor?

12. What passages from the teachings of Jesus stress concern for the poor?

10 The Correlation of Treasure and Heart

"Provide purses for yourselves that will not wear out, a treasure in heaven that will not be exhausted, where no thief comes near and no moth destroys. For where your treasure is, there your heart will be also."

—Luke 12:33b-34

I murdered my brother royally that day. I was about ten, I guess, so he must have been twelve. We had started out having fun together, but the fun ended abruptly when he was a thief.

We were eating purple grapes. I complained that I didn't like the fact that all the good flavor came out first, and, after all the pleasure, a person was left with only skin and seeds in her mouth. So Glen suggested that we squeeze out the juice into glasses and then eat the rest of the skin and pulp. After a while we could drink a few swallows of the delicious juice.

I thought it was a great idea so we immediately set to work, each carefully squeezing out the juice into our separate glasses. I worked hard, all the while anticipating the great pleasure that would be mine when I finally drank the juice. I didn't mind all the dry pulp and skin because the reward would be well worth it.

For a long time I worked, and Glen worked beside me, but he stopped to drink his occasionally. I thought he was stupid, not waiting till the end for one great, glorious moment of pleasure.

It was my own fault for hoarding. Just when I got to the point that I was ready to drink my lovely little quarter-cup of exquisite juice, Glen snatched my glass and drank it all. I killed him with my screams and hate.

So it is with those who store up things for themselves and are not rich in the things that really matter. My childhood happiness was shattered for the day when my treasure was stolen.

I've recounted that incident on other occasions and didn't realize until today how comically it illustrates Jesus' point in Luke 12. No matter what sort of treasures we might lay up for ourselves on earth (even grape juice!) we will find them not able to satisfy our deepest desires. Jesus says, "Make for yourselves purses that are not being worn out." In the Greek the continuing action of that second verb stresses that all the treasures of this earth are constantly in the process of being worn out.

We often fall into the trap of thinking that earthly treasures will indeed satisfy us. We set for ourselves goals and believe that if we can just get to them we will find contentment. It is sad that we do that as Christians even though it could be possible for us to know better. That is why we need constantly to hear this reminder from Jesus not to get caught up in accumulating that which will not last.

Because we live in times when many have rebelled against the materialism of their parents, we might think that we have escaped this danger. And yet the "new bourgeoisie," as Francis Schaeffer calls it, seeks for affluence just as much as the older generation, only in different forms.

Now young people seek for earthly treasure in having enough drugs or alcohol, enough sex or wild parties to satisfy them. Some search for enough popularity or prestige or power. Some Christians search for enough piety!

But thieves and moths come in all sorts of shapes and sizes. Physical goods can be stolen or broken or misplaced, or they can begin to malfunction. What the moths don't get, the mildew will (or the slugs here on the West Coast). It always disappoints me when my favorite clothes that I've made get worn out. I don't want to give them up because of my efforts in making them. Why do things get so important to us?

We must be careful in listening to these words from Jesus, however, lest we put a different "performance principle" in the place of earthly striving. He is not commanding us here to work hard at laying up treasure in heaven. God is not keeping a list of spiritual points so that when we get to heaven we can be rewarded appropriately for the specific number of good deeds we have done during our earthly existence. That would be a whole new sort of law under which to labor.

Christ did not come to impose upon us a new law. He is not saying that we have to work at setting ourselves up for the future life. How horrible it would be if we had to live under that kind of burden in our Christian faith and life.

Don't forget that Jesus has just said, "Do not be afraid, little flock, for your Father has been pleased to give you the kingdom." The words of verse 33 are a response to verse 32, even as verse 34 declares the motive.

Because we have been assured that the Father has already graced us with possession of the Kingdom, we are freed (that is what salvation means!) from any need to strive after it. I can give the whole project up—all my efforts to justify my existence, all my attempts to earn God's favor, all my strivings to be good or to fulfill the law or to be so pious. Now because I am set free by the Good News of grace in Christ, I can respond with love and worship and Joy to the privilege of being part of the Kingdom. I can choose to be involved in the Kingdom plans.

One special way to be involved in the Kingdom is to be part of its program to proclaim the Good News to the begging poor (as we saw in Luke 4:18-19 and 12:33). If I sell my possessions and give in order that they might be taken care of, I will not be accumulating a huge bank account here on earth. But what Joy it will be in heaven when I meet my treasure there—all those persons who have come to participate in the Kingdom more deeply because my treasures have been directed to that end. That purse of Joy in heaven will be unfailing. Jesus has promised that those who participate in the Kingdom will never be snatched from it (John 10:28).

Jesus is inviting us, then, in this verse to avoid having a split heart. The Greek use of the word *heart* means much more than our English heart. We use it symbolically to mean the center of one's emotional life, and so we speak of people suffering from a broken heart or loving from the bottom of one's heart.

More deeply, in the New Testament, the term *heart* stands for the center and source of the whole inner life. As such, it is the basis for one's thinking and feeling and acts of will. When Jesus speaks of where our hearts are, then, He is questioning our total interest. What controls our actions and concerns? How are we focusing our energies and creativity and time, as well as treasures?

In Luke 16:13 Jesus says, "No servant can serve two masters. Either he will hate the one and love the other, or he will be devoted to the one and despise the other. You cannot serve both God and Money." That is the choice recognized also here in Luke 12:33-34. Either our use of material resources will reflect that we are the servants of the Lord, or it will reveal that we are chasing after earthly treasures. It cannot be both. The two attitudes are mutually exclusive.

If I think my possessions are mine alone for myself, I will hoard them as such. If I recognize that they are gifts from God to be used for His Kingdom, then I will make use of them accordingly. The place where our treasure is will reveal where our heart is.

Let us concentrate on that outflow for just a moment. Imagine what our lives would be like if our hearts were so firmly fixed on the Kingdom that every penny of our treasures were directed toward its upbuilding and extension. Think what freedom we could experience if such were the case.

We would not have to worry about how to get enough money. We would know for sure that this promise of Jesus would be fulfilled: "Seek his kingdom, and these things will be given to you as well" (v. 31). We would not be afraid because we would trust that the resources of the Kingdom would always be sufficient for all our needs.

Therefore, we would be able to give away freehandedly. We would be so rich in love that we would know how to give charitably without being obnoxious. We would know how to be tender in our caring for the needy and would assist them in ways that build their dignity and enable them to grow in spirit and freedom.

And if there were enough of us that could give like that, we could deal in earnest with the world hunger problem, and the problem of our ghettos, and the problem of crime that is produced because people don't have enough to survive or to maintain their humanity. We could build a society of free persons, able to pour themselves out for each other because there would never be any want.

Does that sound too idealistic? Yet that is the vision laid out for the Kingdom by the Old Testament prophets as well as by Jesus. It was practiced in the early Christian church, and it worked. Acts 2:42-47 tells us that no one suffered from want because other members of the Body even went so far as to sell their possessions if anyone had need in order that all could share together. In 2 Corinthians, Paul tells the believers that his purpose in asking them to give is not so that they should be shortchanged, but so that each in his abundance can provide for the needs of others and all will have enough (2 Cor. 8:13-15). And isn't his description of the Macedonians delightful, that in their poverty and Joy they gave with liberality? (2 Cor. 8:1-2). Isn't this a marvelous equation: extreme poverty plus overflowing Joy equals rich generosity?

That is the vision for our use of our financial resources. If our hearts are fixed on the Kingdom, we will be excited to be part of making that vision more of a reality in our world.

If our hearts are set on the Kingdom we will not be as concerned for property values as we will want to make sure that everyone has a decent place to live. We will not be as concerned for what is politically expedient as we are for true justice in our laws and courts. We will not be as concerned for getting ours as we will strive for the well-being of all.

One of the challenges in this sentence from Jesus is that an interpretation from the opposite side gives us a way to work on ourselves in the matter of our attitudes about financial stewardship. Not only does it stress that the place of our treasure will indicate the state of our heart, but also it encourages us that where we put our treasure, there our heart will go.

I experienced that once in a very simple way. I had been trying to deal with this correlation of treasure and heart in my own spiritual growth. One day as I was driving back from some graduate courses in theology I was taking at Pacific Lutheran University, I kept worrying about how I would get the money to pay the tuition bill that was coming up. Although I tried not to fret, nagging thoughts persisted in my head. Finally, I thought, *Lord, all this worrying is showing that my heart is in the wrong place. I need to give more to You to get my priorities right again.* So I decided right then that I would send five dollars more out of the grocery budget to feed the hungry somewhere. That decision felt good, and the rest of the drive home was remarkably pleasant and free from anxiety.

You can imagine my surprise, then, when I returned to a mailbox containing two checks, both for work that I had done for free (I thought) for some churches several months before. Their total amounted to more than I needed to pay the tuition bill, give a tithe, and cover the extra money I had decided to give away.

We can't outgive God. The delightful thing about our relationship with Him is that He has many surprises for us when we get our priorities straight. I don't mean that we can manipulate Him in these terms: give to God and He will give you more back. But when our hearts are fixed on His Kingdom, He will indeed faithfully provide for all of our needs.

That is not to put a law over us again. It is a principle that invites our participation. If we are having trouble fixing our hearts on the Kingdom, the truth will help us to invest in it more.

Where my treasure is, that is what I pray for. That is one of the most significant factors in the fixing of my heart because God frees my attitudes so much during prayer times. If I am investing some of my grocery money in feeding the hungry through the sponsorship of a child, I will pray for that child regularly. I care more and more what is happening to Yin Man and Jessy. They are becoming such precious children to me! My heart is becoming more and more fixed on desiring the Kingdom of God to happen mightily in their lives.

We will pray more for our churches when we are more serious about the tithes we give to them. We become more involved when we start to be concerned about how the congregation is spending the money we are investing.

If we really take seriously, then, where our money is going, we will become much more involved in the ways in which the Kingdom is happening in this world. That leads to some exciting prospects for ministry and service and prayer.

For example, right now I am specifically frustrated by the way my local congregation spends its money. I haven't seen much concern for the poor. I got angry (righteously, I think) when we spent hundreds of dollars for silver communion ware (I thought the pottery was beautiful) while people are starving. Now that I'm frustrated about it, I can get involved in doing something about it, particularly in this case working to start some mission groups in the parish to be more practically and intensely concerned about our involvement in the world as the people of God.

And the concern for the unemployed in our midst that I told you about in a previous chapter led to some practical action in my church at Thanksgiving when a special offering was taken to help those families without work. I share those examples not to pat myself on the back, but to stimulate your own thinking about what might be an appropriate response to Christ's invitation to you.

We need to be immensely practical about these verses in Luke 12. The Christian is not called to an empty asceticism, which in most cases turns out to be another means of self-glorification, just another way to live under the performance principle. Instead, Christ calls us to wise use of our possessions. The concept is stewardship.

If I am a good steward of what I possess as well as of what I am and what I am becoming, I will want to invest in that which will expand my heart, or contribute to my wholeness. Francis Schaeffer speaks against the super-spirituality that causes people to reject their culture and take on a pseudo-mystic asceticism.

The gospel of Luke especially helps us to see that we are not called to be totally separate from the world. We respond to the grace of Christ by being more fully involved in the world. But we must keep the world out of us. I don't want to get trapped in the world's value systems.

A Christianity without beauty, music, art, or poetry, is not the fullness of life to which Christ calls us. But those things must be under His lordship. Therefore, I will use my possessions and my gifts and my creativity to draw others to Him and to deepen His presence in me. Marjorie

Holmes has written a lovely book that describes all the ways in which God comes to her. *How Can I Find You, God?* describes His use of such things as reading, work, nature, prayer, and the arts to draw the authoress closer to Himself. We know from the Scriptures that God's specific objective revelation of Himself is the best and clearest way to know Him, but we close out some of His Joy if we devalue all the other gifts He might use.

All of these comments are intended to help us realize that the placing of our treasures is a very complex issue. It is not that I simply dump all my money into the church coffers and expect that then I have my priorities straight. On the other hand, to give nothing into the treasuries of the Lord calls the state of my commitment into question.

I can't get away from this chapter without also putting in a word for the daily quiet time, a most important part of our stewardship and a means by which we can think through the other dimensions. Our time is a treasure, too. If we spend some of it reading God's Word and meditating and praying, our hearts will be there with the treasure and with Jesus. I love Brother Lawrence's simple description of our goal: to practice the presence of God. If we spend some treasured moments in our days practicing His presence, our hearts will rest in Him all the rest of the time, too.

Questions for Personal Application

1. How can we avoid making the sentence, "Provide for yourselves purses . . ." into another law?

2. What do I think our treasures in heaven involve?

3. How have I experienced the corruption of thief or moth when I have missorted my treasures?

4. How have I seen in my life that where I put my money affects the state of my heart?

5. How has the reverse been true in my life—that when I applied my treasure somewhere the heart followed after?

6. What specific plans would I like to make with my family for readjusting the investment of our treasure?

7. How do I understand the connection of verses 32 to 34 in Luke 12?

11 The Delight of Christ's Surprises

"Be dressed ready for service and keep your lamps burning, like men waiting for their master to return from a wedding banquet, so that when he comes and knocks they can immediately open the door for him. It will be good for those servants whose master finds them watching when he comes. I tell you the truth, he will dress himself to serve, will have them recline at the table and will come and wait on them."

—Luke 12:35-37

I was sure they were all dead. The final shootout had looked so real. The movie had caught me so completely in its web that the ending took me totally by surprise.

I'll never forget the movie, *The Sting,* because of that surprising conclusion. Just when I thought the cheaters had finally been caught in their own games, I realized that the final shootout with the police, too, had been a staging. They rose from their playing-possum deaths, had a good laugh, and went on with business as usual. The cleverness of it all turned everything upside-down. All the old values and expectations just didn't apply any longer. Although I don't remember the details of the movie all that well, I can still feel the awe of that sudden twist, the delight of that surprise reversal.

Jesus must have sent the same kind of delight through the bones of His listeners as He told the parable of this text, for its ending is far more surprising. As in many of His parables, Jesus turns all our expectations upside-down and tells us, "This is the way it is in the Kingdom of God." The modern expression, "blows my mind," is the best description of what this reversal does to my thinking. All the old categories, all the past insights are knocked away in the glory of this reversal.

Imagine: the master comes to serve his slave! That is absolutely unheard of in the Oriental culture. A slave was the master's possession, totally dedicated to the will, and even petty whim, of his master. Jesus even uses that relationship later in Luke to teach us that we don't have any right to expect any reward from our master. When we have worked diligently in the fields and then come in to serve our master his supper, we have only done our duty (Luke 17:7-10).

In this parable from chapter 12, however, Jesus asserts that the slave is treated as an honored guest. We can just imagine how the listeners must have reacted.

"Come on, Jesus, You're pulling our leg."

"That's the silliest thing I ever heard."

"No way! It doesn't happen like that in real life."

Was Jesus contradicting Himself? Had He lost His mind? What could be the meaning of this strange twist? Surely Jesus wasn't serious about such a reversal.

The seeming contradiction of these two parables in Luke 12 and 17 gives us the opportunity to learn some important skills in biblical interpretation. The paradox forces us to look very carefully at the context of both of the parables and to consider their historical setting in order to determine more accurately their meaning. Only after we have done diligent work in exegesis are we free to draw some conclusions about how these parables might apply to our lives as Christians in our times.

The teaching context of the two parables allows them to come to opposite conclusions and still both be true. In the case of the story from Luke 17, Jesus is teaching His disciples about the importance of obedience. He was warning them to watch themselves so that they would not be the cause of another person's sinning (v. 3). Causing another to sin is such a grievous danger, He warns, that it would be better for a person to have a millstone wrapped around his neck as he was thrown into the sea. It is such a terrible thing to be the cause of another's sin that a sure death would be vastly preferred. That is an incredibly strong warning for believers to be aware of their influence.

Next Jesus urges His disciples to be faithful about forgiveness. If the offender sins against you even seven times (the biblical number for completeness), still forgive him. In other words, even if he sins against you to the point of exasperation, still forgive him. Even if you doubt his honesty that he should keep on sinning against you and then keep on coming back for forgiveness, still forgive him. The question is not the state of that person's repentance. The question is your willingness to forgive. So keep on forgiving.

When the disciples hear that injunction, they react as I think we would. They cry out to Jesus, whom Luke calls "Lord" in this place, "Increase our faith!" (v. 5).

But Jesus' response is surprising. He says, "If you have faith as small as a mustard seed, you can say to this mulberry tree, 'Be uprooted and planted in the sea,' and it will obey you" (v. 6). That is a phenomenal picture, too. The mulberry tree was the most deeply rooted of trees. If any plant could be selected to depict hardiness, the mulberry would be a good choice. But Jesus declares that if we just speak to it that it should be uprooted, it will obey.

Why does Jesus tell such a strange story here, when the disciples have just asked Him to increase their faith? The point is strongly made: it is not a question of how much faith one might have; the question is whether or not one is obedient. We don't have to try to grow our faith; we need instead to learn to be obedient to what faith we have. Forgiveness of those who offend us (even up to seven times) does not depend upon the extent of our faith. It requires merely that we obey the One who calls us to forgive as He forgave.

Then, when that point is clearly made, Jesus continues with the parable that seems to contradict our text from

Luke 12. He says,

> "Suppose one of you had a servant plowing or looking after the sheep. Would he say to the servant when he comes in from the field, 'Come along now and sit down to eat'? Would he not rather say, 'Prepare my supper, get yourself ready and wait on me while I eat and drink; after that you may eat and drink'? Would he thank the servant because he did what he was told to do? So you also, when you have done everything you were told to do, should say, 'We are unworthy servants; we have only done our duty.' "
>
> Luke 17:7-10

We can't pat ourselves on the backs because we have become such wonderful forgivers. We have done only what we were called to do. We can't think we are so great if we avoid causing offense to others and do not lead them into sin. We are just being what we should be as the people of God.

The picture is one of a little Semitic farm. The master probably has only one slave, and that slave must do everything. It is his responsibility to tend the fields, watch over the sheep, fix the dinner, and serve it to his master.

This parable calls us to recognize our total unworthiness as the people of God. That we should have the privilege of serving is a magnificent thing. Certainly when we look at our responsibilities seriously, we will recognize that we don't deserve any thanks. We are only doing our duty when we complete our tasks.

We are not able to forgive seven times. We are not able to avoid causing others to sin. We are not able to be obedient to the faith that we have. Our unworthiness is a fact that we must face.

The parable in Luke 12 seems to begin in the same way. Jesus calls us to diligence as we wait for the coming of the master. Our version renders the beginning of the story with this command: "Be dressed ready for service" (v. 35).

The original Greek says literally, "Let them be of you the waists having become girded." The construction of this sentence is extremely awkward and, therefore, highly significant. The imperative of the verb meaning "to be" together with the perfect participle, which stresses that an action decisively begun continues to be the case, pictures for us a state of readiness. One should have his long robes pulled up into the belt around his waist so that he is constantly ready for action.

There is also an emphasis on the possessive "of you." That construction seems to be saying, "It doesn't matter what is happening to anybody else. Just make sure that your robes are girded up at all times."

I love long, flowing robes, but I don't run well in my long dresses. They look very graceful and full of splendor, but they get in the way if a person needs to be ready for action. People in the time of Jesus would tuck their long outer robes into a belt when they needed to move quickly. That is the image Paul refers to when he tells us to have the belt of truth firmly about our waist (Eph. 6:14).

So this story seems to begin like the one in Luke 17. We should be ready for our duty, dressed for action at all times. And then that picture is reinforced by a second image: "Keep your lamps burning" (v. 35).

This image brings to our minds the story of the ten virgins, which occurs only in the gospel of Matthew. There the foolish virgins were shut out of the wedding feast when the bridegroom appeared because they had failed to come prepared to keep their lamps burning (Matt. 25:1-13).

Similarly, Jesus warns His listeners in this story to keep their lamps burning so that they can be "like men waiting for their master to return from a wedding banquet, so that when he comes and knocks they can immediately open the door for him" (v. 36). Wedding banquets lasted for an indeterminate length of time. If the servants were to be ready upon their master's return, they must be prepared for anything. No one had any way of knowing when he might return.

Scholars argue over whether or not this story refers to the final *parousia,* or coming, of Christ. They debate the question of how much teaching about His return Jesus actually did. They speculate about the hearers of this story; were they the disciples or the crowds? Was it addressed to the Pharisees and other rulers of the church of those days? Was Jesus warning against an imminent disaster or crisis, or was He speaking about His own return at the end of time?

Because Jesus instructed His disciples about His coming again at other times recorded for us in the gospel of Luke, I think He was referring to His own coming when He told this story. He invites constant preparedness for those who would follow Him as they await His return.

But we can't discount the possibility that this story also refers to any visitation from God. He has all sorts of surprises up His sleeves (if He has sleeves!) that we will miss if we are not prepared for them. When we are all dressed and ready for service, sometimes God pulls a quick reversal and blesses us soundly.

I experienced that tonight. It has been a tough day. I've been trying to get some studying done for a retreat I'm leading next weekend. I've also been very concerned all day for a friend who is in trouble. Some other projects had to be done for my work, too, and then we had a "family meeting" for this community in which I live. Next, one of the members of the community wanted to talk with me about some struggles she is going through trying to find herself and what kind of work she wants to do in her life.

Finally, all the distractions were removed, and it was time for me to be able at last to work on my writing. I was eager to work on this chapter and was just about to begin typing when the telephone rang. At first I hesitated selfishly, not wanting to be bothered. Most people who call me late at night call for help and counseling. I needed to ask God to get my attitudes right so that I would be willing to help whoever was seeking my aid.

What a nice surprise it was when the call turned out to be a gift. A good friend was calling from Seattle to tell me some good news. Our conversation was delightfully uplifting, and her words, "You are so special," gave me some love that I had been longing for all day. God's grace came to me richly in that surprise reversal. What I had expected to be work turned out to be blessing instead.

Those surprise twists come to us from God much more often than you or I realize. This parable invites us to open our eyes to be more observant, to recognize that the Master comes and serves us in many special ways throughout our days. And someday He will come with the greatest grace surprise of all.

The decisive factor is our readiness. Jesus continues, "It will be good for those servants whose master finds them watching when he comes." The original Greek uses the word for "blessed." That blessedness is so important that Jesus says the phrase twice, "It will be good for those servants" (again in v. 38). Many wonderful things can happen in our lives if we are watching for them.

Just *how* good it will be Jesus goes on to say. "I tell you the truth, he will dress himself to serve, will have them recline at the table and will come and wait on them." The craziness of that image catches us again. Unbelievable! The Master will actually gird Himself to serve. He will cause them to recline (probably with a lot of protestation on their part). And having come beside them, He will serve. Can we ever get over our surprise at such grace?

This strange picture is in keeping with the way Jesus defined Himself and how He lived out His ministry. When the disciples argued over who would be the greatest at the time of the betrayal of Jesus, He rebuked them with these words:

> "The kings of the Gentiles lord it over them; and those who exercise authority over them call themselves Benefac-

> tors. But you are not to be like that. Instead, the greatest among you should be like the youngest, and the one who rules like the one who serves. For who is greater, the one who is at the table or the one who serves? Is it not the one who is at the table? But I am among you as one who serves."
>
> Luke 22:25-27

A few sentences later Jesus tells His disciples that He will confer His kingdom on them, just as the Father had conferred it on Him, and they will be able to "eat and drink at my table in my kingdom and sit on thrones, judging the twelve tribes of Israel" (Luke 22:30).

Not only will the Master come to serve us, but He will give us the privilege of participating with Him in the reigning as well. We are indeed lifted up to share His place in the heavenly realms (see Eph. 2:6).

Ever since first reading this parable I have been awed by its majesty and overwhelmed with the humility with which we must respond. How could we be so blessed as to receive such a privilege?

While I was preparing to write this chapter, the importance of this declaration hit me in a new way. I had never realized before until now that, in contrast to Matthew and Mark, Luke does not very often record these words of Jesus: "I tell you the truth." The Greek says literally, "Amen, I say to you." Only in six places does Luke use that phrase, and each one is in the context of a major statement about the Kingdom of God. To look at those six statements increases our wonder at the immensity of the grace Jesus bestows upon us.

The first occurrence of that phrase in Luke takes place when Jesus is teaching in the Nazareth synagogue, and He says, "I tell you the truth, no prophet is accepted in his home town" (4:24). His statements at that time raised the wrath of His former neighbors, and they took Him out to the cliff with every intention of throwing Him over.

But also at that time Jesus initiated His ministry in a

decisive way. He had come to fulfill the words of the prophet Isaiah and to do the work of the Kingdom —proclaiming good news to the poor, healing the sick, setting the captives free. Those who were not part of that Kingdom would be alienated by what Jesus did and said. He would not be received by His own kin. Truly, one dimension of the Kingdom is that its message is hard to receive.

The third usage of that phrase (after the one we have been studying in chapter 12) occurs in the 18th chapter. The disciples had been rebuking those who brought children for Jesus to touch them. With all the authority of His Word, He contradicts them and says, "I tell you the truth, anyone who will not receive the kingdom of God like a little child will never enter it" (18:17).

Only with the acceptance and belief of a child can one enter the Kingdom. Its grace is too hard to figure out; the gift of the Master serving is too hard on a person's pride. Only in the humility of a trusting child can the surprise of the Kingdom be received.

Later in that same chapter comes the fourth instance of the "I tell you the truth" phrase. As the disciples observe the rich man going away sorrowful because he couldn't follow Jesus' instruction to sell all in order to give to the poor, Jesus declares that camels could pass through the eye of a needle more easily than a rich man could enter the Kingdom. In astonishment the crowds ask Him, "Who then can be saved?" And Jesus answers, "What is impossible with men is possible with God" (18:26-27).

Peter is quick to announce his renunciation of all things in order to follow Jesus, and the Lord immediately assures him, "I tell you the truth, no one who has left home or wife or brothers or parents or children for the sake of the Kingdom of God will fail to receive many times as much in this age and, in the age to come, eternal life" (18:29-30). Truly, the coming of the Master to serve His servants involves not only the blessings of eternal life, but also the rich treasures of the abundant life made available to the people of the Kingdom now. Those statements about the Kingdom are stupendous.

In the fifth usage of the "I tell you the truth" phrase in Luke, Jesus calls His followers to be watchful and careful, lest they allow themselves to be pulled away from the Kingdom by the anxieties of life. Disciples must maintain a constant vigilance, and their faithfulness in the Word is the discipline that will keep them in the Kingdom. Jesus says, "I tell you the truth, this generation will certainly not pass away until all these things have happened. Heaven and earth will pass away, but my words will never pass away" (21:32-33). That means that what He has said about the Kingdom is for sure. Earthly things are only temporary, but the Kingdom is for real. Eternally real.

Jesus was about to undergo the suffering that would make the fulfillment of His words about the Kingdom possible. Those who heard Him would be witnesses of those things. And we still live in the midst of the signs of the age that Jesus has described. We still have not seen the one sign of the end, the very appearing of Christ in the clouds. Meanwhile, the ages continue to pass, but this age remains the same. These times are characterized by the shaking of the heavenly bodies, distress in the land, wars, and rumors of wars. All those things continue to take place. But someday, the sign of the end will appear. Jesus will come again, and all who have believed His "I tell you the truth" comments about the Kingdom will be received to Himself.

One such example is the thief on the cross. Jesus' final use of the phrase "I tell you the truth" in the gospel of Luke occurs when He assures the thief, "Today you will be with me in paradise" (23:43).

That is as much of a surprise as the parable before us. The kingdom is open to everyone, including thieves. The

Master will come and serve them, too.

Together those six sections seem to me to give all the secrets of the Kingdom. It is available to all those who are not offended by the words of the Prophet Jesus, to all who receive His grace as children. To them He will give both abundant and eternal life, and they will receive it in this time as well as beyond time. Today all those who hear Him will receive His gift of paradise: He will indeed come to them and wait on them.

Will wonders never cease? Love so amazing: we want to respond to it by selling our possessions and giving to the poor. We want to have ourselves all dressed and ready for service. We want to be careful not to let our lamps go out so that we are ready when He comes. The reversal of our fortunes is sealed with all the authority of God Incarnate, who says, "I tell you the truth."

Years ago I learned a poem by George Herbert that catches this wonder far better than any words I could compose. That saintly priest gave us the following gem, based on this text from Luke:

Love (III)

Love bade me welcome; yet my soul drew back,
        Guilty of dust and sin.
But quick-eyed Love, observing me grow slack
        From my first entrance in,
Drew nearer to me, sweetly questioning,
        If I lacked any thing.

"A guest," I answered, "worthy to be here":
        Love said, "You shall be he."
"I the unkind, ungrateful? Ah, my dear,
        I cannot look on thee."
Love took my hand, and smiling did reply,
        "Who made the eyes but I?"

"Truth Lord, but I have marred them: let my shame
Go where it doth deserve."
"And know you not," says Love, "Who bore the blame?"
"My dear, then I will serve."
"You must sit down," says Love, "and taste my meat":
So I did sit and eat.[1]

Questions for Personal Application

1. How do we keep our loins girded up? How do we keep our lamps burning?

2. What have been some special times in which the Master has come to serve me?

3. Why are the contexts so significant for our study of these two parables that seem to contradict each other?

4. How do we see an even deeper impact when we compare the six places in Luke where he records these words of Jesus: "I tell you the truth"?

5. Why does Jesus' Word carry so much authority?

6. How does this chapter make me feel?

7. How do I experience the blessedness of the Master's serving me now?

1. George Herbert, *The Selected Poetry of George Herbert,* ed. Joseph H. Summers. The Signet Classic Poetry Series, ed. John Hollander (New York: New American Library, 1967), p. 255.

12 The Blessedness of Being Prepared

"It will be good for those servants whose master finds them ready, even if he comes in the second or third watch of the night. But understand this: If the owner of the house had known at what hour the thief was coming, he would not have let his house be broken into. You also must be ready, because the Son of Man will come at an hour when you do not expect him."

—Luke 12:38-40

I was embarrassed! I was living alone, so usually there was no need to clean up my projects in order to avoid getting into someone's way. It had been a busy week. I was working on a writing project and plans for an upcoming retreat. Too busy. I had not taken the time to do the dishes for several days. I'd gotten out a big box of Christmas decorations to find one thing that I wanted to put up for Advent, but the rest of the box was spread out on the floor. The place was chaos.

And then my friend came for a visit. There wasn't even a chair for her to sit on. I couldn't make her feel welcome at all. My home was a disaster.

If I had only known she was coming! I could have cleared a space in at least one of the rooms and thrown all the clutter behind closed doors. But suddenly she arrived, and there was no escape. If only I had been ready!

How many times have you said that? Probably you have been embarrassed in situations for which you were not prepared. Perhaps you have had some frightening moments because you were not ready for some exam or event. We all understand how much better it is to be ready. That is why we easily nod our heads in agreement when Jesus speaks here of the blessedness of being ready.

The Greek construction emphasizes the blessedness more than our English versions do. Together with verse 37, the verse that begins our text forms a saying that surrounds the unusual twist on which we concentrated in the last chapter, and that saying both begins and ends with "blessed."

The version quoted above doesn't use the word *blessed,* but chooses the phrase, "it will be good," instead. Unfortunately, the concept of "blessedness" has been terribly watered down in our contemporary Christian circles because the term is often overused and used abstractly. "It was such a blessing," and "that really blessed me," and other such phrases have become trite because they can be used to mean almost anything.

When Jesus uses the term *makarios,* He means a specific state of being, defined by many associations with the word in its usage. Originally in its usage in classical Greek, the term meant to be free from daily cares and worries. In a way, that connotation still exists in its scriptural forms, but the New Testament occurrences add many other dimensions to the meaning of the word.

Of the fifty instances of the word in the New Testament, Luke has more than any other book. Most of those occurrences are in the Sermon on the Plain, which parallels Matthew's Sermon on the Mount in many ways. In the lists of Beatitudes in those two sermons, the pronouncements of blessedness give a reason for, or a description of, the bliss under consideration.

As *The New International Dictionary of New Testament Theology* points out, the Beatitudes are not so much descriptions of various virtues ordained by God, but all of them point to different aspects of the same attitude. As the world nears its end, those who belong to the Kingdom, those who have received the gift of salvation, are able to maintain an attitude of patience and hope. The statements of the Beatitudes are paradoxical. For example, the fact that the Kingdom belongs to the powerless or the sorrowful contradicts the attitudes of the world and our usual expectations. But blessedness is therefore seen to be wrapped up in salvation, which in turn is wrapped up in the coming of the Kingdom of God and is, moreover, inseparable from Jesus, who proclaims it and makes it possible.

Blessedness occurs in both the future and the present. Luke's version of the Beatitudes even stresses immediacy in phrases such as "Blessed are you who hunger now, for you will be satisfied" (6:21). In other words, the blessedness lies not only in the future comfort and reward, but also in the radical effect on life-style contained in the present.

That is why it appeals to me to remember that the classical Greeks used the term *makarios* to mean freedom from cares and worries. Those who are caught up in the Kingdom, those who are actively involved constantly in seeking it (as we described the life-style associated with Luke 12:31), don't worry about their poverty or their powerlessness.

When we apply this understanding to the verse before us, we can understand the blessedness of those who are ready more thoroughly. Not only are the servants waiting for their Master appropriately blessed when He comes because He will gird Himself and seat them to dine with His service, but also they are blessed now because their life-style is different while they are waiting.

The key is our attitude in the waiting. A few years ago, Jeannette Clift George, the actress who played Corrie ten Boom in *The Hiding Place,* taught me an important lesson about waiting. She had spoken at a women's retreat that I was attending, and I was so caught by one of her comments that I ran to the platform to discuss it with her when she concluded her speech. She had talked about the holy restlessness in our lives and what to do with it. At that time I was haunted by a deep desire to teach the Scriptures to crowds of young people—not so much because I wanted to do it, but because I really wanted young people to get excited about God's Word and the place it could have in their lives and faith.

As I talked with Jeannette about that constant desire in my deepest being, she said that such ambitions from the Lord should be nurtured in preparation for the day when the vision would come to pass. "But while you are waiting," she emphasized, "use the time to prepare."

That was tremendous advice. Not only did the times of preparation make the waiting more endurable, but also the study was an important part of getting ready so that, when the opportunity arose, I could take it with Joy and run with it.

That same lesson must be planted deeply in the core of our beings as we wait for the return of Christ. Our longing for Him is a good one, a holy restlessness that we do not want to quench. But sometimes the longing is so intense it seems intolerable. We must learn to let that pain drive us more fervently into using the time to prepare. How can we prepare for His coming?

How many persons do you know that are not ready for Him yet? How much more of your time could be spent in telling others what His coming involves?

If, as the Beatitudes stress, our blessedness lies in having a different attitude toward the world, part of our preparation also involves clearing the world's values out of our systems. And that is where the classical Greek definition for *makarios* is so appropriate. If we are using the time of waiting to prepare, we will be free from the worries and anxieties of the world around us. The need to accumulate wealth, possession, power, and prestige will not afflict us. Our goals will be different.

Jesus calls us to a constant state of readiness, a life-style that exhibits the values of the Kingdom while it is still in the process of coming. The parable says that the servants who are ready are blessed indeed if the master comes at the second or third watch. Although the Roman legions had four watches, the Jews had three. The second watch occurred around midnight, and the third was the early morning watch. Jesus invites us to be ready for the Master's coming all through the night and into the new day. That is a fitting picture of our wait for His return.

We go through times of dark night as we wait for His return. And how blessed we are indeed when we can be faithful to the Kingdom during those difficult times. But we must not give up on the Kingdom either when brighter days come. Sometimes the ease of our lives lulls us into non-vigilance, and then the values of the Kingdom get diluted by those of the world into which we have slipped.

I should be careful lest I allegorize this parable too much. We do the story form injustice if we match up each little aspect of the texture with the realities of life. The point of the parable is that we are to be ready at all times, whether the world around us is in darkness or light.

After the double emphasis on blessedness, Jesus switches the imagery to make His point another way. Now in an excellent example of the overdrawn illustration of Eastern humor, Jesus warns against slipping up at any time and allowing one's house to be broken into. We can just imagine someone sitting up all night to make sure that no one gets in to steal his stereo.

We smile when we hear this parable because, of course, no master of any household could know at what time of day the thief would come. The advantage a thief has is the suddenness and the surprise. Homes in Jesus' day were made of mud bricks, so the picture is one of a thief digging through the walls. If the master were alert he would hear the sounds of the thief. But he must be there and ready when he comes.

This parable offers a good example of the danger of allegorizing. I have heard Christians interpret this story in terms that conveyed the opposite meaning of its intention because they tried to match up the fabric of the story point for point with the truth of reality. It is wrong to say that the thief is Satan and that he digs into our hearts to steal the treasure of the Kingdom of God. And we must be prepared at all times to prevent his doing that so that when Jesus comes, we will be ready to receive Him.

When Jesus tells the parable, He is not referring to Satan, but to Himself. Lest it shock us that He chooses a morally corrupt figure to represent Himself, we must remember that in several parables He does that. We will avoid misinterpreting if we stress again that a parable normally makes one and only one point. Here the point of the parable is the suddenness and unexpectedness of the coming. Thieves are the best illustrations of that in our society. It is not that Jesus will come back to steal anything from us (although the way some Christians walk around with gloom about their faith, one might think that is the case). This parable doesn't address any other questions except the one concerning the time of Jesus' return. And in keeping with all His other teaching on that subject, Jesus here again merely stresses that it will be a surprise, so we should at all times be ready.

The image of a thief to represent His sudden coming must have really struck His disciples because they used it in several other places in the New Testament. Both Peter and John as well as Paul use the image to speak of the Last Day.

In Peter's second letter he reminds his readers that although it seems like a long delay before the coming of the judgment, Jesus is being patient before His return to allow everyone to come to repentance, since His desire is that not anyone should perish. He will come, however, Peter warns, as a thief. "The heavens will disappear with a roar; the elements will be destroyed by fire, and the earth and everything in it will be laid bare" (2 Pet. 3:10b). Since that is the case, Peter continues, how should you then live?

Peter's next injunction fits in well with Jesus' words in our text in Luke. He tells his readers how to be ready for the coming of the Master, how to have a life-style of constant readiness that both anticipates the coming of the Kingdom and lives its reality during the waiting time. These are his instructions:

> "You ought to live holy and godly lives as you look forward to the day of God and speed its coming. That day will bring about the destruction of the heavens by fire, and the elements will melt in the heat. But in keeping with his promise we are looking forward to a new heaven and a new earth, the home of righteousness. So then, dear friends, since you are looking forward to this, make every effort to be found spotless, blameless and at peace with him. Bear in mind that our Lord's patience means salvation."
>
> 2 Peter 3:11b-15a

John's uses of the thief imagery occur in the book of Revelation, at first in the fifth of the letters to the churches, the one to Sardis. There, too, the context speaks of judgment in connection with the thieflike coming of Christ. But the message to the church at Sardis also praises them that there still remain a few "who have not soiled their clothes. They will walk with me, dressed in white, for they are worthy" (Rev. 3:2-6). These are the ones whom the Master will find ready whether He comes in the second watch or the third.

Later, in the sixteenth chapter of his visions, where John records the pouring out of the seven bowls of wrath, just before the seventh angel pours out the last great plague, the Lord says, "Behold, I come like a thief! Blessed is he who stays awake and keeps his clothes with him, so that he may not go naked and be shamefully exposed" (Rev. 16:15). The key to being prepared for the sudden coming of the Lord with the unexpectedness of a thief is to stay awake. Blessed indeed will be those servants whom the Master will find awake (Luke 12:37).

The apostle Paul's use of the thief imagery comes in an extended discussion in the first letter to the Thessalonians about the coming of the Lord. This is the section in which he comforts his readers with the assurance that those who have died will be gathered together with the rest when Jesus comes again. He stresses that we can encourage each other with our words about the fact that we will be gathered together in the clouds to meet the Lord in the air (1 Thess. 4:13-18).

Then he continues with very important instructions for how we should spend our time in the meanwhile. He writes these exhortations:

> "Now, brothers, about times and dates we do not need to write to you, for you know very well that the day of the Lord will come like a thief in the night. While people are saying, 'Peace and safety,' destruction will come on them suddenly, as labor pains on a pregnant woman, and they will not escape. But you, brothers, are not in darkness so that this day should surprise you like a thief. You are all sons of the light and sons of the day. We do not belong to the night or to the darkness. So then, let us not be like others who are asleep, but let us be alert and self-controlled. . . . But since we belong to the day, let us be self-controlled, putting on faith and love as a breastplate, and the hope of salvation as a helmet. For God did not appoint us to suffer wrath but to receive salvation through our Lord Jesus Christ. He died for us so that, whether we are awake or asleep, we may live together with him. Therefore encourage one another and build each other up, just as in fact you are doing."
>
> 1 Thessalonians 5:1-11

One of the things that I love about Paul's letters is that he always couples his words of warning with warm words of encouragement. He also stresses the need for improvement along with a pat on the back. Notice his advice for the way to handle the surprise of the thieflike coming of the Lord. It won't surprise us, he says, if we always live like people in the day. If we are on guard during all the watches, we will be ready. God's plan is not for us to be caught without expectation. If we keep looking, instead, toward the coming again of Christ, we will always be ready. And the way we prepare for the coming of the Kingdom is by living by the Kingdom's values now. That is why we are to be involved in encouraging one another and building up one another, even as we have been doing.

That is also the conclusion Jesus stresses after the parables of our text. He says, literally, "And you yourselves, be becoming ready, for in the hour you do not think, the Son of Man is coming" (v. 40, author's translation). Several aspects of that conclusion are significant for our consideration.

First of all, the Greek imperative is in the continuing present tense. To get ready for the Lord's return is not something that we can do once and for all and then think that we are prepared. No, rather, we are always in the state of becoming ready and therefore will always be ready. The injunctions of Peter and John and Paul all emphasize this same thing: that the process of becoming ready is what fits us to be ready. God's plan is for us to be part of the Kingdom. If we are choosing to live in anticipation, we are being readied. That takes us back to where we began, for the essence of the word *makarios* is that the blessedness anticipated for the end time is experienced to some extent in the changed life in which we participate now because of that anticipation. The Kingdom is always an eschatological reality if we are in the process of seeking it; we have it somewhat already, but not yet in its entirety.

Second, we must stress again that we will never know the hour when the final fulfillment will take place. We live in an age when various cults and groups think that they have the final times pretty well pinned down. It is significant that in Luke 21, Jesus gives all sorts of signs of the times and only one sign of the end. Many persons misinterpret those signs and think, because the signs of the times are being fulfilled, that we are approaching the end of the world. They forget that those signs of the times have been in the process of being fulfilled since Jesus was here on earth. There have always been wars and rumors of wars, signs in the heavens, and men's hearts failing them for fear.

When Mount St. Helens blew its stack, many people thought that the volcano was a sign that Jesus will soon be back. Perhaps He will. But Christians have been thinking that for 2000 years. I believe that He could come back tomorrow. I wish that He would come back today. But I also think that He might not come back for a long, long time. He is the One who declared that He waits to give everyone a chance for repentance.

Whenever He comes, there will be only one sign of the end, and that is when He Himself appears. Meanwhile, the signs of the times keep happening. We keep seeing wars and earthquakes and volcanoes, and their purpose is to keep reminding us that we live in an age that is not characterized by the dominion of the Kingdom of God.

Yet someday that Kingdom will be ushered in, in its totality. Someday Jesus will come back. Meanwhile, we have no basis for trying to pin down the time when that will happen, contrary to all the dates and timetables of various heretical groups. Scripture is quite clear about that fact.

Finally, the Greek text of this fortieth verse concludes with the statement, "The Son of Man is coming." What a grand conclusion! I am always sorry that our English translations don't duplicate the ordering of the Greek text. The main emphasis of this verse is not that we won't expect Him. I think that the Greek ordering stresses the main point that the Son of Man is indeed coming.

Unfortunately, some churches no longer think that this is an important part of our theology. Because Jesus has been so long in coming, the fact that He will come loses its dramatic effect. I was even criticized once in a denominational church for emphasizing the longing with which we anticipate the return of Christ.

I think such longing is a most fitting response. We live in a broken world. Someday Jesus will return and institute His Kingdom in which all brokenness will be healed; tears will be dried; sorrow and sighing will flee away. It is appropriate behavior to weep and to yearn now.

In our next chapter we will consider our actions more intensely to discover together how we must live out the meanwhile. But for now it is important for us to remember this major fact in our faith and existence: Jesus is coming back.

That fills us with Joy. And it also accentuates the sorrow of the meanwhile. We must keep the two in a healthy tension. We keep them in balance by means of our awareness of the blessedness in which we live. We are blessed because, as we wait for the return of the Master, we have a different attitude toward this life. We are set free from its anxieties and cares and worries. We are freed instead to concentrate on being alert, self-controlled, awake, righteous, blameless, spotless, at peace with Him.

Jesus' disciples understood that when He first gave this exhortation. And they passed His encouragement on to others in their letters. And in those letters, finally, they exhorted us to encourage one another and build one another up with these words. Just as we have been doing, let us do it even more.

Questions for Personal Application

1. What does the word *blessed* mean to me?

2. What does the need for constant readiness mean in my daily life?

3. How do I feel about Jesus' use of a corrupt figure to

picture Himself?

4. What encounters with other groups have I had in which the coming again of Jesus was misunderstood?

5. How can I handle the false teaching of those who pin down the time of Christ's return?

6. What do I want specifically to change in my life to be ready for Christ's return?

7. What aspects of my life are ready for His return? (This question anticipates the discussion of the next chapter.)

13 To Be Faithful and Wise Stewards

"Peter asked, 'Lord, are you telling this parable to us, or to everyone?'

"The Lord answered, 'Who then is the faithful and wise manager, whom the master puts in charge of his servants to give them their food allowance at the proper time? It will be good for that servant whom the master finds doing so when he returns. I tell you the truth, he will put him in charge of all his possessions. But suppose the servant says to himself, "My master is taking a long time in coming," and he then begins to beat the menservants and women-servants and to eat and drink and get drunk. The master of that servant will come on a day when he does not expect him and at an hour he is not aware of. He will cut him to pieces and assign him a place with the unbelievers.

" 'That servant who knows his master's will and does not get ready or does not do what his master wants will be beaten with many blows. But the one who does not know and does things deserving punishment will be beaten with few blows. From everyone who has been given much, much will be demanded; and from the one who has been entrusted with much, much more will be asked.' "

—Luke 12:41-48

It happens all the time in school. If the teacher has to leave the classroom and assigns certain responsibilities to be fulfilled in her absence, some of the students will be very diligent to work on those tasks, while others will use the situation for goofing off. Those who are faithful are the ones that the teacher will choose the next time for certain responsibilities, and the more thoroughly they complete them, the more willing she will be the next time to entrust them with tasks that require more care.

Students who goof off, on the other hand, must be disciplined. If not, the teacher knows that the next time their misbehavior will be worse. It is important to deal with rebellion as lovingly and constructively as possible, but that does not allow the teacher to be permissive. If the teacher herself really cares about her students, she will want them to develop habits of obedience and diligence.

That is the reason for the stories in this section of Luke 12. Most scholars see that Jesus answers Peter's question in terms that are especially meant for the leaders of the church. In His time the Lord addressed His words to the disciples, but as Luke recorded them he must surely have seen how applicable they were also to the situations the first Christians were experiencing in the developing church. Jesus had prepared for what would happen with His people and had warned them ahead of time against the dangers of bad stewardship in the responsibilities entrusted to those who became leaders.

Consequently, His words in this section are particularly vitally needed in the church of our time. You who are reading this book are called to be leaders in your church by the very fact that you care enough to study the Scriptures. Whatever the type of leadership you exert (even those of you who work very quietly behind the scenes), these words from Jesus call you to a special awareness of the privilege, responsibility, and challenge of your ministry.

I wonder which of the two parables Peter was referring to when he asked the question that begins this section. If he was thinking about the one that immediately precedes his interruption, he might be asking about the nature of the responsibilities of the disciples. Then his question would mean, "Jesus, are we to be more watchful than others? Are You giving that warning to watch primarily to us or to everyone?"

But if he was referring to the previous parable, the one in which the master pulls the great surprise and waits on his servant, then Peter's motive for asking could be much different. In that case, his question fits the pattern that we see so often in the pre-Pentecost Peter. He would in essence be saying, "Lord, are we disciples going to have that special privilege of being served by the Master, or does that apply to everybody?''

Perhaps his question involves both. We don't know for sure because Jesus doesn't really answer directly. Instead, He responds with another question that calls Peter to take proper stock of what it means to be a disciple in the first place. The way Jesus answers seems to stress that the issue is not to what a person has been called; the issue is not whether or not a person is among the chosen twelve. Rather the issue is how that disciple *responds* to his call.

It is significant that Peter addresses Jesus as Lord and that Luke uses the phrase, ''The Lord answered.'' That title is not used often in Luke. Its usage here seems to accentuate that Jesus is talking about the disciple's response to the issue of His lordship. He asks, ''Who, then, is the faithful manager, the thoughtful one?'' What will distinguish the disciple who handles his trust with dedication and wisdom?

The question makes us think. Of course, its answer lies in the very question itself. The faithful and wise steward is the one who acts faithfully and wisely. Now we must ask for ourselves if that description fits our discipleship.

The details of the parable weave a texture that pictures the faithful and wise steward. His task in Semitic culture was to oversee the whole estate of his owner. Usually he was a slave like all the rest of the servants, but to him was entrusted the managing of his master's affairs to free the master from all the routine duties of administration. Because of the nature of those tasks, the steward had an unusual degree of freedom of action and, therefore, as we shall stress later, a corresponding burden of responsibility.

If this steward was faithful and wise, the affairs of the estate would run well. Particularly in this parable Jesus describes the steward's responsibility as that of giving the food allowance to other servants at the proper time. Obviously, if the manager did that job well, the rest of the household staff would be much happier, and, consequently, all the affairs of the estate would be run with greater effectiveness.

There is a dangerous tendency for us to allegorize this parable and say that the household staff stands for the other members of the church under the responsibility of the head elder or leader or pastor or whatever. The food allowance, then, could correspond to the administering of the sacrament, or the giving of the nourishment of the Word, or any of all the other jobs that are parts of the administrative authority of the stewards of the church.

But to allegorize in such a way causes us to understand this parable too narrowly. We must keep the picture quite open. Its texture pictures the whole atmosphere of the church and everything that is involved. If Jesus is teaching this parable to warn the leaders of the church that will develop after His death, His story calls them to full-hearted dedication in all matters. He has asked, "Who then is the faithful manager, the thoughtful one?" That question has too many applications for us to tolerate too confining of a systematization.

What is the quality of our discipleship as we await the *parousia*? Jesus says the servant is "blessed" whom the Lord finds doing his job when He comes. In fact, He goes on to stress, by means of an introductory "I tell you the truth," that the master will promote that servant. This introductory formula doesn't have quite as much emphasis as the one we considered in chapter 11, but it does stress the factual nature of this conclusion. (It is unfortunate that the New International Version translates the two phrases identically since they are different in Greek.)

The point is that the reward for faithfulness is greater responsibility. That appeals to the core of each of us, for deep inside we like the challenge of greater tasks. We all need something with greater purposes and meaning to live for.

That realization urges me to pause for awhile in our exegesis of this text to apply this parable particularly to our lives as God's people. I'm sure that you, too, have often struggled with frustration at the little jobs you've been given in the Kingdom. Sometimes we wonder why we can't just do something major. It is important for us always to be reminded of the necessity for faithfulness in the smaller tasks in order that we might prove ourselves able to handle the larger ones.

It is not that God has to check us out first to see if we are capable of the greater jobs. He knows us inside out; He designed all the capabilities we possess, of course. It is not a question of our abilities, but of our attitudes. Our faithfulness is on the line. If we are not diligent and eager to do the lesser things, then what might be our motives for doing the greater? Do we want those tasks for the advancement of our own fame or prestige or personal sense of worth? Or do we desire to serve in larger ways because of our commitment to the Kingdom? If the latter is the case, that commitment will be just as eager to do the less noticeable jobs. Our true character will be revealed by the way we handle the "food allowance" that must be administered at the proper time.

Jesus paints the other side of the possibilities very darkly before coming to some conclusions in this parable. He says, literally, "But if that servant might say in his heart, 'My lord delays to be coming,' and begins to strike the servants and the maidservants and to be eating and drinking and to be drunk, the lord of that servant will have come in a day in which he does not anticipate and in an hour which he does not know and he will cut him in two and his part with the faithless he will place" (vv. 45-46, author's translation).

The details of the story create a strong picture of contrast to that of the steward who is faithful to his job of dispensing the food allowances. Instead of caring for the other servants, he is described as totally wrapped up in himself.

If he is a careless steward, the long delay of his master might lead him to begin to indulge in his own pleasure. Instead of feeding the servants, he beats them. Instead of dispensing food for others, he hoards it for himself, and in the debauchery of his eating and drinking is found to be drunk.

The master's response to such a situation is appropriately severe. When he returns unexpectedly and finds his steward irresponsibly indulging in his lusts, he will cut him in two and place him among the unfaithful. The picture is necessarily harsh. Luke's record uses a rare word that stresses the severity of the punishment.

Again, we must not allegorize and think that we can pin down specifically what this means in application to the life of a disciple who has gone astray. For example, it is dangerous to say that this expression of cutting in two means that the unfaithful one will be cut off forever from Christian fellowship. The point of the parable is simply that punishment is just and duly meted out.

Similarly, we cannot conclude that the second part of the warning means that the unfaithful disciple will be cast with the unbelievers into hell. Then we would all suffer with terror, for at various points in our lives we have all been unfaithful to our responsibilities.

Rather, we must remember that Jesus was speaking primarily to His disciples. To warn them that their part might be cast with the unfaithful if that is how they behave is to hit them right where they need to be bothered. We dare not slip into taking our discipleship for granted. We must not begin to think, because we are the chosen and beloved of God, that we can allow ourselves to indulge in our pleasures to the exclusion of our responsibilities toward the other servants and to the master of the household himself. The warning is simply a statement about the certainty of punishment to those who fail to be God's people as He has called them.

Scholars who believe that this parable is addressed to the church of Luke's day say that verses 45 and 46 picture the dark side of the church. In fact, one commentary on Luke asserts that the details of the parable correspond to the situation in Corinth, with which Luke would have been familiar because of his close association with Paul. And indeed the picture in 1 Corinthians 11:21 and other places shows some relationship of details.

I think we do an injustice in our biblical interpretation, however, if we think that Luke just put this parable in because he was trying to say something to the churches of his day. Far more accurate to our understanding of the Scriptures is the realization that Christ's Word speaks appropriately in His own time as well as prophetically to other times.

Isaiah had addressed the same sorts of problems among the people of God in his day. Isaiah 5 warns against those who look after themselves and indulge in their own lusts while the poor are destroyed (see especially verses 7 to 14). The prophet's words, as well as those of Jesus, warned the disciples in His time, as well as in Luke's time and in our own, that to degenerate into bureaucratic control violates our call to be stewards of God's many-sided grace.

The point of the parable is clear. Each one of us must check out our own faithfulness. Do we deserve the master's wrath and punishment or wealth and promotion?

Now in the last two verses of this section Jesus establishes some basic principles. His statements have caused much anxiety among Christians who wonder whether He means that there are different levels of punishment or different heights of reward in the afterlife. Again we must be careful not to read more into the text than is there. An awareness of the Jewish-thought context in which Jesus spoke can also help us to interpret His words more accurately.

Many passages in the Old Testament show us that there is in the Scriptures a distinction between sins that are committed unconsciously and those that are intentional. For example, in Numbers 15, the offerings for unintentional sins are clearly spelled out in verses 22 to 29. When atonement has been properly made for such sins, they will be forgiven.

However, the chapter continues, "But anyone who sins defiantly, whether native-born or alien, blasphemes the Lord, and that person must be cut off from his people. Because he has despised the Lord's word and broken his commands, that person must surely be cut off; his guilt remains on him" (vv. 30-31). This distinction seems to correspond to the difference between speaking a word against the Son of Man and blaspheming against the Holy Spirit, as was discussed in chapter 4 of this book.

Similarly, the psalmist asks forgiveness for both kinds of sins in Psalm 19. "Who can discern his errors?" he asks and therefore pleads, "Forgive my hidden faults." Then he continues, "Keep your servant also from willful sins; may they not rule over me. Then will I be blameless, innocent of great transgression" (Psalm 19:12-13).

As Romans 1 and 2 point out, there is not such a thing as basic ignorance of God's law. It has been written into the hearts of men (see especially 1:20 and 2:14-15). Thus, everyone is responsible before God for the actions of his or her life. But those who have greater understanding also have a greater responsibility to live from that insight. The prophet Amos records the word of the Lord, saying,

> "You only have I chosen
> of all the families of the earth;
> therefore I will punish you
> for all your sins."
>
> Amos 3:2

Because they are especially chosen to know the Lord, they

bear a greater burden for their failure.

James emphasizes the same culpability when he declares, "Anyone, then, who knows the good he ought to do and doesn't do it, sins" (James 4:17). We can't escape the conviction of our knowledge.

This conclusion seems to indicate that Peter's question, which began the whole discourse on responsibility, was asked to determine if only the disciples would receive the preferential treatment of the master serving the servants. Jesus answers, then, by saying, "That may be the case, but it is far more important for you to realize that the special place for which you have been chosen demands of you significant responsibility."

Verses 47 and 48a can be summarized as follows: the one who knows, but willingly sins (either by omission or commission), will be punished severely. The one who does not know, but sins, will be punished sparingly. Sin is worthy of punishment, whether or not the person did it consciously.

On the other hand, Jesus declares the positive principle at the end of verse 48. He says, literally, "But to each one who has been given much, much will be sought from him, and to whom much has been entrusted, greater shall be asked him." That principle corresponds to Jesus' earlier words in Luke 8:18. There He urges the disciples to "consider carefully how you listen. Whoever has will be given more; whoever does not have, even what he thinks he has will be taken from him."

Those declarations could be seen as the arbitrary decisions of an unjust God who plays with people according to His whim. But we know that they are uttered in the same context as the story about the master serving his slave. Because we know the Lord as the Teacher, Healer, Reconciler, Enabler, Giver, Provider, and Surpriser that He has revealed Himself to be, we know that His call to responsibility is fair and just and right.

That is for the disciple a great source of comfort as well

as a warning. We are urged to make the most of our talents and gifts, to use what we have to the best of our abilities. But we are also set free not to have to be more or other than what we are. We don't have to fulfill our responsibilities as anyone else fulfills his. We can indeed be true to ourselves.

In his *Commentary on Luke,* Ray Summers presents clearly the import of this principle of "responsibility, requirement, and retribution." He distinguishes it as follows:

> It [verse 48] has been frequently understood as teaching degrees of reward and degrees of punishment (because of the preceding two illustrations). This represents a human sense of justice—among those to be rewarded, some clearly deserve greater reward than others, and among those to be punished, some clearly deserve greater punishment than others. We often tend to seek in the Scriptures specific answers to specific questions when the Scriptures contain, not specific answers, but general principles. If this passage is to be applied to final rewards and punishments, it must be on the basis of general principle. In application of that principle it may be well to include the idea of *capacity for* the bliss of heaven or the woe of hell. One may anticipate enjoying the bliss of heaven to the extent of his capacity to enjoy it, though he may lack the capacity of a Jeremiah or a Paul. In the Scriptures such matters as these are left in the wisdom and love and power of an infinite God. God, not finite man, will determine the ultimate issue.[1]

I especially appreciate Summers' conclusion that these matters are left in the hands of God, who is infinitely wise to handle them. I often think that if Jesus were to walk among us today He would tell us to quit worrying about whether there are degrees of rewards or punishment and to get on with the business of being faithful to our calling. The point is not how much I should fear God's greater wrath. The point is that I should recognize that my gifts

1. Ray Summers, *Commentary on Luke* (Waco: Word, 1972), p. 163.

and knowledge call me to make use of them. They have not been given to me to waste.

That makes me want to get very personal with you, dear reader. I wish I could know you as an individual, see your gifts, and understand the ways God has called you. Then I would want to spend time talking with you, just the two of us, to discuss what God is doing in and with our lives. God in His sovereign wisdom has gifted each of us with a special combination of attributes that no one else possesses. You are accountable to Him to find out and do His will. So am I.

One very excellent book concerning this subject is *Knowing God's Will* by M. Blaine Smith and published by InterVarsity Press. I recommend it highly for those who want to discover more truly the nature of their calling.

I am grateful for the experiences and the friends and the biblical instruction that God has given me to help me find how best I might serve Him. Just in the last year the CEM board has helped me in many ways to find out what I should be doing with my time and efforts. But now that I am more aware of those things, I feel an extra responsibility to be faithful in doing them.

That is not a burden. In fact, is it the very opposite. We err greatly if we see these principles in the mouth of Jesus as calling us to an oppressive life of compulsion to fulfill our tasks and duties. No, much to the contrary, it is a thing of great Joy. When we use our gifts to the utmost, we find such filfillment and satisfaction, such a deep sense of the presence of God, such a thrill in being in the center of His will, that we really don't want it any other way.

Even as I type these words, my fingers are flying over the keys. It is such a profound excitement for me to put down these meditations for you. I believe that this is the task for which I am called at this moment. And so it is not an onerous duty to write.

The apostle Paul deals with this principle from Jesus

also in his first letter to the Corinthians. I would recommend that you study 1 Corinthians 3:10—4:5 in your personal quiet time. The conclusion that he reaches after all his exhortations to be fitting as the temple of God and to recognize the source of everything in God is an excellent reminder for us as we close this discussion on the parables of Jesus. He warns his reader not to judge others and stresses that when the Lord comes He will bring to light what is hidden and will expose the things that are in men's hearts (sounds like Luke 12:3!). Then he declares, "At that time each will receive his praise from God" (1 Cor. 4:5).

That is our motive for being faithful to our calling. What matters above all—in fact, the only thing that matters at all—is that we please the God who loved us so much that He already fulfilled everything for us. We are only stewards of His gifts and possessions. The only thing required is that as stewards we be faithful. His praise has already been secured for us. Remember this: it has been His good pleasure to give us the Kingdom.

Questions for Personal Application

1. Why do I think Peter asked the question of verse 41?

2. How conscious do I think Luke was of the application of these words from Jesus to the situation in the church of his time?

3. In what ways do I feel good about my own faithfulness?

4. In what areas of my life do I see that I have not been very faithful or wise?

5. What do I want to do about those areas? (Please be careful that you don't fall into some works-right-

eousness or self-help programs that deny grace.)

6. What do I see as the particular strengths with which I have been entrusted?

7. How can I use those strengths more effectively?

14 Reading the Signs of the Times

"I have come to bring fire on the earth, and how I wish it were already kindled! But I have a baptism to undergo, and how distressed I am until it is completed! Do you think I came to bring peace on earth? No, I tell you, but division. From now on there will be five in one family divided against each other, three against two and two against three. They will be divided, father against son and son against father, mother against daughter and daughter against mother, mother-in-law against daughter-in-law and daughter-in-law against mother-in-law. . . .

"When you see a cloud rising in the west, immediately you say, 'It's going to rain,' and it does. And when the south wind blows, you say, 'It's going to be hot,' and it is. Hypocrites! You know how to interpret the appearance of the earth and the sky. How is it that you don't know how to interpret this present time?

"Why don't you judge for yourselves what is right? As you are going with your adversary to the magistrate, try hard to be reconciled to him on the way, or he may drag you off to the judge, and the judge turn you over to the officer, and the officer throw you into prison. I tell you, you will not get out until you have paid the last penny."

—Luke 12:49-59

Even the little children know how to read the fog in Olympia. The young daughter of one of my friends surprised me one morning when she said, "It's going to be a sunny afternoon." How did she know? "Whenever the fog looks like this, it will burn off by noon." She was right.

We live in an age of frequent crises in world affairs. Suddenly hostages were seized in Iran; suddenly Afghanistan was invaded; conservatives won major landslides in the elections. Astute observers of those and similar situations had predicted them, but most of the rest of the world paid no attention to their warnings. Then in retrospect we all said, "We should have seen it coming." We need to learn to read the signs of the times.

In the final section of Luke 12 Jesus urges first the disciples and then the whole crowd to pay attention to the signs of the times. He wants them to be alert to the critical nature of His coming. His appearance is indeed a decisive turning point in history, as well as in the lives of individuals. We must learn to understand His moment as well as we can read the sky.

Our breakdown of Luke 12 into chapters in this book has a major disadvantage in that it fragments the progression of thought in the narrative of Jesus' teaching as Luke has recorded it. The words of Jesus to His disciples in verses 49 to 53 must be read in light of the previous emphasis on the accountability of those who are the stewards of the mystery of the gospel. From everyone who has been given much, much will be demanded, and from the one who has been entrusted with much, much more will be asked. What is asked of those who have knowledge might cause division rather than peace. Jesus did not come to bring ease and softness, but fire and intensity of commitment. It was not easy for Him, furthermore, to bring the gospel; it necessitated suffering and death on His part.

Here in Luke 12 He expresses keen awareness of the future of His ministry and the recognition of what He must undergo. This first paragraph under our consideration involves both an explanation to the disciples of His requirements and a challenge to them to prepare for those requirements.

Verses 49 and 50 are almost identical in pattern. First Jesus makes a statement about the nature of His ministry, and then He declares His eagerness to bring that to completion. We can understand more deeply the victory of His cry from the cross, "It has been brought to the finish!" (John 19:30, author's translation) when we hear the longing of these verses.

Jesus was no ordinary prophet. One of the worst things

contemporary philosophy does to Jesus is call Him a great teacher. That softens to extinction the crucial confrontation that His life must bring to the lives of those who observe Him. The Greek of verse 49 says literally, "I came to throw fire upon the earth."

The people around Him should have been prepared for such a ministry. John the Baptizer constantly declared that the One coming after him would baptize in the Spirit and with fire. "His winnowing fork is in his hand," John declared, "to clear his threshing floor and to gather the wheat into his barn, but he will burn up the chaff with unquenchable fire" (Luke 3:17). In this verse we see clearly that that fire is a symbol of judgment.

Earlier, John had said that it was time for such judgment. "The ax is already at the root of the trees," he warned, "and every tree that does not produce good fruit will be cut down and thrown into the fire" (Luke 3:9). Because Jesus' ministry involved so much healing, so many acts of deep compassion, it is easy to forget that His major purpose was to confront men's lives with the need for repentance and forgiveness so that they might find new life and salvation in Him. That necessitates death—to one's pride and the entire previous way of life.

The background to both the message of John the Baptizer and Christ's fulfillment of it comes from the second half of the book of the prophet Malachi. In chapters 3 and 4 Malachi records the announcement of God that He will send His messenger to prepare the way, and John knew that he was the fulfillment of that prophecy. Then, the Lord declares that He Himself will come to His temple. Who can endure this coming, He asks, "for he will be like a refiner's fire" to purify the priests (Mal. 3:1-4).

In the fourth chapter all the people are included in the judgment of the day of the Lord. In that day, "It will burn like a furnace. All the arrogant and every evildoer will be stubble, and that day that is coming will set them on fire," says the Lord Almighty. "Not a root or a branch will be left to them. But for you who revere my name, the sun of righteousness will rise with healing in its wings" (Mal. 4:1-2).

I love the promise of that second verse. Along with the judgment of the day of the Lord, there is the good news of healing and purifying and victory. So also in the words of Jesus. His assertion that He has come to throw fire does not stand alone, for He is eager for it to be kindled. The fire will involve purifying—yes!—but such refining is intended to purify for the Lord a people for His glory.

The fire of judgment must be borne by Jesus Himself, however, if men who believe in Him are to be spared its punishment. That is why Jesus continues in verse 50 by saying, "But I have a baptism to undergo." From the Psalms we learn that water signifies deep agony. In Psalm 42 we read these lines:

> "Deep calls to deep
>   in the roar of your waterfalls;
> all your waves and breakers
>   have swept over me."
>
> Psalm 42:7

Similarly, Psalm 69 contains this image:

> "Save me, O God,
>   for the waters have come up to my neck.
> I sink in the miry depths,
>   where there is no foothold.
> I have come into the deep waters;
>   the floods engulf me."
>
> Psalm 69:1-2

What is exciting to us as Christians is the recognition that because Christ willingly bore that baptism the whole image of water changes its meaning for us. He submitted to its necessity even though it remained a choice that He would have avoided if that had been possible. Because of

His willing acceptance of it, baptism becomes for us a means for the drowning of the old life in order that the new might be resurrected.

Even as Jesus would have wanted to choose another route, so we also often balk at the death to ourselves that our baptisms must entail. We are not willing to bear the fire of purifying or the waters of agony. But because of the dedication of Christ to His task for us, we are enabled to want to follow in His steps.

That choice on the part of Jesus has been decisively noted by Luke prior to this text. In chapter 9, after Jesus had responded to Peter's confession that He is the Christ by foretelling His own suffering and death and resurrection; after He had revealed His glory to the three disciples on the Mount of Transfiguration; after He had settled an argument among the disciples over who would be greatest by declaring that the least among them was indeed the greatest; then Jesus decisively set His face to go to Jerusalem. That resolution on the part of Jesus is the hinge for the remainder of Luke's gospel. Thereafter, inherent in all Jesus' actions is the sense that Jesus is going, going, always going toward Jerusalem and the inevitable baptism of death that awaits Him there. The culmination of it all is that which is forecast by the rest of Luke 9:51—that Jesus set His face to go to Jerusalem "as the time approached for him to be taken up to heaven."

Now in chapter 12 we see intensely how much that resolution affected the course of Jesus' thoughts and deeds. Here in verse 50 He says, "And how distressed I am until it is completed!" Perhaps a better translation of the adjective would be the word *constrained.* The Greek word from which it is translated means to be "hard-pressed, pushed together, constrained possibly by circumstances." Whenever the word is used in the New Testament, it means a total absorption into something, a complete investment in whatever occupies one's attention. Luke uses the same word in Acts 18:5 to describe Paul's exclusive devotion to preaching to the Jews that Jesus was the fulfillment of their expectations for the Messiah.

Jesus had set His face to go to Jerusalem, so now He was constrained by the desire to finish that task to which He was committed. Paul set his face, too, and he devoted himself ceaselessly to the task of trying to convince the Jews and then the Gentiles that Jesus had finished the task to which He was committed. Paul invites us into the same constraint. In 2 Corinthians 5:14 he writes, "for the love of God constrains us" (Revised Standard Version).

We are invited, too, to set our faces to go to Jerusalem, to enter into the baptism of death to ourselves. The process will be difficult for us, too, Jesus warns. He doesn't want us to have false expectations, so He asks next in Luke 12, "Do you think I came to bring peace on earth? No, I tell you, but division" (v. 51).

That statement summarizes the great paradox of the Christian life, for the coming of Jesus into our lives ushers in the deepest of peace as well as the dissension for which He prepares us. William Danker, in his comments on verse 50, compares Jesus to the philosophers who say that we were not born to be happy so therefore must get on with the work. Danker puts into the mouth of Jesus this invitation: "Let us squander our lives in the opportunity of disaster."[1]

That is an incredible statement and an excellent capsulization of the message of Jesus as it applies to our lifestyles. The freedom of the gospel invites us to pour out our lives for others, to recognize even in the most horrible of situations the opportunity to serve. That is the truth that enables us to bear the division that the cross entails. Yes, Jesus does give us that infinite peace that passes under-

1. William Danker, *Jesus and the New Age: A Commentary on the Third Gospel* (St. Louis: Clayton, 1972), p. 155.

standing. Absolutely, He gives us peace in our relationship with God. But the result in human relationships might be disagreement, and terribly painful disagreement at that. In even the coziest of relationships, those of the family, division will come.

Jesus pictures this household of five: the father, the mother, the son, the son's wife, and the daughter. When the cross confronts them, some will respond and others will resist. Three will be set against two and two against three. It seems to be a generational split—the father and the mother against the son, his wife, and the daughter, but we dare not press that observation too far. The point of the illustration is simply that some of our deepest human bonds will be broken if we are bound to Christ.

It is not that Jesus wants such division to happen. He doesn't willfully produce it. But when men and women make choices, their decisions will be disruptive to those who want things to stay the same. The gospel is revolutionary. It will radically alter the lives of those who are constrained by it. There will no longer be casual acceptance of the status quo, for those who are seized by the gospel will recognize the need to bring the Kingdom to bear on this world.

To that world Jesus now turns. After all the intense conversation with the disciples about their responsibility and the challenge of their calling, Jesus now addresses the crowds. He commends them for the accuracy of their weather forecasting. (Perhaps we need a few of their weathermen in our day!) Of course, when the clouds rise in the Mediterranean sky, a person knows that rain will come. And the south wind over Palestine brings the hot desert air, so the temperature inevitably increases. Such forecasting of the earth and sky would be easy.

Jesus seems to imply, however, that interpretation of the times should be just as accurate. He calls the crowd hypocrites, for they concentrated only on that which was superficial and did not pay attention to those things that really mattered. The crowds were not able to see the true significance of their own times because they did not want to. It really was not a matter of being unable, but of being unwilling.

That emphasis strikes me hard today. I've been working through an excellent book on how to find the Lord's will in order to be more helpful to some persons who are struggling with some major life decisions right now. Yesterday I read a chapter that stressed that our problem usually is not that we don't know the Lord's will, but that we aren't really ready to follow it. As I wrestled with that chapter, I recognized how painfully much that is true in my own life.

That is true both with sins of omission and with those of commission. We know what God's will is in most temptations, but we commit the sin anyway because we don't really want to follow His plan. If we did want to, we would have the strength available to us to fight the temptation. On the other side, we know that it is God's will for us to have more care for the poor, for example, but we don't really want to follow His will if it means giving up a bit of our comfort and complacency.

Now especially we must recognize that rebellion in regard to the signs of the times. We live in an age desperately in need of committed Christians willing to bear the pain of division and responsibility in order to present to the world the challenge of the gospel. Everyone around is looking for purpose in our days. People feel uprooted by rapid change; many can find no meaning in the frenzy of indulgent activity that characterizes our society. How will we help them learn to examine the significance of the times?

It was my privilege last summer to study the gospel of Luke at the Lutheran seminary in Berkeley under the teaching of Dr. David Tiede from Luther Seminary in St.

Paul, Minnesota. Dr. Tiede presented to us the theory that Luke wrote his gospel after the fall of Jerusalem in order to help his readers know for sure that their belief in Jesus was not misdirected. The fall of Jerusalem was not the fault of the Christians; rather, Jesus had warned the Jews about that fall throughout His ministry. Christians could be confident in the face of the massive confusion that Jesus still remained the Lord over history, that He was, indeed, the Lord for the meanwhile, that time in between His ascension and His coming again.

For many reasons too numerous to detail here, that theory appeals to me. It causes many of the details in Luke's gospel to make more sense. Particularly here at the end of the twelfth chapter the theory is relevant to our interpretation of the text.

If Jerusalem had been destroyed and the Jews were blaming the Christians, it would have been very important to remember that Jesus had warned the Jews about their failure to recognize what was happening in their midst. Because they failed to accept Jesus for who He really is, their position as the people of God continued to be lost. Meanwhile, their external habits of religion continued to be characterized by the hypocrisy against which Jesus preached so often in the gospel of Luke. And that same pretension prevented them from understanding the meaning of the life of Jesus. They did not accept the message He came to bring.

But Jesus did indeed warn them. Here He asks, literally, "Why do you not know how to examine this time?" The word *time* chosen here means more than simply the particular chronological moment. It points, rather, to the critical moment in Israel's history. Their response to Jesus would decide their destiny. Those who chose to believe in Him could recognize His lordship even in the meanwhile, even when all of life around them didn't make sense.

The application to our lives in contemporary society is extremely relevant. We still live in an age of the meanwhile. Much of the old life around us has fallen. Former values regarding sexuality, the family, the place of God in daily life are discarded. How do we go on in a mixed-up world?

We can go on—and even go joyfully, in fact—because we know who is the Lord of the duration. While we wait for Jesus to return, we know that to believe in Him is the most reasonable response to the facts of His life and death and resurrection.

All the signs of our times point to the fact that the world cannot get along without Him. That both confirms us in our convictions and constrains us to reach out lovingly to those who don't yet know the truth of His coming.

How will we respond to our times? The final parable of Jesus in Luke 12 gives us some advice. Again we must be very careful not to allegorize. Some folks like to pin down who the judge and the magistrate and the officer are. But all those details work together to create the texture of the story, which makes one and only one point.

Its point is this: it is much better to try to handle things before they get to the state of needing a court decision. The parable is a call for wisdom in settling difficulties with one another in view of the crisis that is impending.

One of the commentaries that I studied in preparation for my lectures on Luke last year allegorized this parable unmercifully. The writer thought the details stood for the two different court systems of the Jews and the Romans and concluded that we should not be lulled into a false sense of security. Although we think things are going all right here on earth, we have a hopeless situation in our case before God. Ultimately, this commentator declared, we cannot avoid God's jurisdiction over our affairs.

I think to contort the parable in that way detracts from its emphasis. Jesus tells the story to crowds that He has just blasted as hypocrites because they don't know how to interpret the signs of the times. He urges them to pay attention to the realities of their situations. The key to the parable is in His introductory comment, "Why don't you judge for yourselves what is right?"

In light of the signs of the times, what is the right thing to do? How can we be prudent and wise stewards of the grace of God? All the parables of this chapter in Luke fit together into a whole. Their points call us to be faithful in our responsibilities, to recognize that if we have been given much, we also have much to give. Rather than get caught unexpecting (having to pay the last penny, according to this last parable), it is so much better to be doing what the Master has instructed us to do so that when He comes He will bid us be seated and will serve us.

Jesus is not telling this last parable as a nice little proverb, a tidbit of advice to teach us how properly to handle lawsuits. The point is much larger than that, a principle much more applicable to all the situations of our lives. Jesus tells us to use as much wisdom in the handling of our affairs as we would use to settle accounts. To solve an issue with our adversaries by means of the magistrate and the judge and the officer would involve a lot of time and hassle and risk. We could avoid all that if we settled out of court with a personal reconciliation. Perhaps we could summarize the point of this story by urging that we do what is right and avoid the hassles.

That might sound like a tremendous oversimplification, but it is, rather, a large principle that can guide many of the details of our lives. It is a call to good stewardship of who we are and what we have, both time and possessions. I think that is especially fitting in light of the times.

If Luke was written after the fall of Jerusalem, the call for wisdom is particularly significant. In light of the strain of the world situation on the people Luke addresses, Jesus' story inviting wisdom would be especially important.

The same is true for us. We live in a terrifying age. It is a critical time for history. Either the people of God will call the rest of the world to repentance and renewal, or the church will continue to slide right into the culture and pass away into oblivion. Either we will affect the world vigorously as we proclaim the truth in Jesus Christ as Lord, or we will be seriously affected by the world. Either we will join Jesus in the fire and baptism, in the division of those who understand His critical importance, or we will never know the peace that He came to bring. Either we will take stock of the times, or we will continue as hypocrites to fail to acknowledge the totality of commitment required by His call.

Either we will be servants failing to fulfill the requests of our Master, or we will be guests of honor when the Master returns and begins to serve. Either we will be seeking the Kingdom, or we will have to run after all the things that the pagan world runs after. Either we will acknowledge Him before men, or we will not be acknowledged before the angels of heaven.

All these are our choices, but they are not made out of fear. They are made on the basis of promises, this one especially: "Do not be afraid, little flock, for your Father has been pleased to give you the kingdom" (v. 32).

All the promises of this chapter, all the exhortations, all the invitations are based on this focus: that the Father really wants us to belong to His Kingdom. Jesus underwent all the suffering of His baptism in order that we might be spared the fire of punishment. That is why we can freely choose the values of His Kingdom. And we can know *for sure* that as we keep seeking that Kingdom we shall know a Joy inexplicable. We will know so much Joy that we will want always to be committed to the values of the Kingdom and to spreading its Good News wherever we go. We will want to sell our possessions and give to the poor. We will want to give much, for we have indeed been given much.

And the result of that committed discipleship will be an even greater abundance of Joy. That is what it means to be the flock of God.

Questions for Personal Application

1. What do the images of fire and baptism mean to me?

2. How do I understand the tension of Jesus as He longed for His baptism to be completed?

3. How have I experienced the division of which He speaks?

4. How have I been right in judging the times?

5. How have I misunderstood?

6. What is the meaning of the final parable in Luke 12?

7. How does the parable fit in with the rest of the chapter?

8. How would I summarize the major teachings of this entire chapter from Luke?

9. Why are the ideas of this chapter so significant for our discipleship?

10. How have I grown since I began studying Luke 12?

11. How do I understand this chapter as it fits into the rest

of the gospel of Luke?

12. What are my goals and visions for future growth in my discipleship?

Appendix A
Resources on Helping the Poor

I. Sections from the Scriptures that emphasize care for the poor
   A. Leviticus 25
   B. Passages throughout the book of Deuteronomy
   C. Isaiah 61 and its fulfillment in Luke 4
   D. Passages throughout the books of the Old Testament prophets, especially Jeremiah, Hosea, Amos, and Ezekiel
   E. Matthew 25:31-46
   F. Passages from the first six chapters of Acts describing the life-style of the early Christian church
   G. The book of James

II. Contemporary reading resources
   A. Hancock, Maxine. *Living on Less and Liking It More*
   B. Lappe, Frances Moore. *Diet for a Small Planet*
   C. Longacre, Doris Janzen. *More-with-Less Cookbook*
   D. Mooneyham, W. Stanley. *What Do You Say to a Hungry World?*
   E. O'Connor, Elizabeth. *The New Community*
   F. Perkins, John. *Let Justice Roll Down*
   G. Sider, Ronald. *Living More Simply: Biblical Principles and Practical Models*
   H. Sider, Ronald. *Rich Christians in an Age of Hunger*
   I. Simon, Arthur. *Bread for the World*
   J. Snyder, Howard. *The Community of the King*
   K. Wallis, Jim. *Agenda for Biblical People*
      (Jim Wallis is also the editor of *Sojourners* magazine, 1309 L Street N.W., Washington, D.C. 20005)
   L. White, John. *The Golden Cow: Materialism in the Twentieth Century Church*

III. Agencies to Support
   A. Bread for the World, 235 East 49th St., New York, New York 10017
   B. Food for the Hungry, P.O. Box E, Scottsdale, Arizona 85252
   C. Lutheran World Relief, 315 Park Avenue South, New York, New York 10010 (almost every denomination has a similar agency)

D. MAP International, P.O. Box 50, Wheaton, Illinois 60187
E. Prison Fellowship, P.O. Box 40562m, Washington, D.C. 20016
F. Death Row Support Project, 2821 McCain Rd., Jackson, Michigan 49203 (You can write to a person on death row by asking for a name.)
G. Voice of Calvary, 1655 St. Charles Street, Jackson, Mississippi 39209
H. World Concern, Box 33000, Seattle, Washington 98133
I. World Vision International, 919 W. Huntington Drive, Monrovia, California 91016

Appendix B
Resources for Studying Luke

Danker, Frederick W. *Jesus and the New Age: A Commentary on the Third Gospel.* St. Louis, Missouri: Clayton Publishing House, 1972.

Franklin, Eric. *Christ the Lord: A Study in the Purpose and Theology of Luke-Acts.* Philadelphia: The Westminster Press, 1975.

Marshall, I. Howard. *Commentary on Luke.* The New International Greek Testament Commentary, edited by I. Howard Marshall and W. Ward Gasque, vol. 3. Grand Rapids, Michigan: William B. Eerdmans Publishing Company, 1978.

Morris, Leon. *The Gospel According to St. Luke.* The Tyndale New Testament Commentaries, edited by R.V.G. Tasker, vol. 3. Grand Rapids, Michigan: William B. Eerdmans Publishing Company, 1974.

Richards, Larry. *U-Turn: Dr. Luke's Guide to a New You.* Wheaton, Illinois: Victor Books, 1973.

Summers, Ray. *Commentary on Luke.* Waco, Texas: Word Books, 1972.

Wilcock, Michael. *Savior of the World: The Message of Luke's Gospel.* The Bible Speaks Today, edited by John R.W. Stott and J.A. Motyer. Downers Grove, Illinois: InterVarsity Press, 1979.

Also Cited

Brown, Colin, ed. *The New International Dictionary of New Testament Theology.* Grand Rapids, Michigan: Zondervan Publishing House, 1975.

Herbert, George. *The Selected Poetry of George Herbert.* Edited by Joseph H. Summers. The Signet Classic Poetry Series, edited by John Hollander. New York: The New American Library, 1967.

Stendahl, Krister. *Paul Among Jews and Gentiles.* Philadelphia: Fortress Press, 1976.

CHRISTIAN HERALD ASSOCIATION AND ITS MINISTRIES

CHRISTIAN HERALD ASSOCIATION, founded in 1878, publishes The Christian Herald Magazine, one of the leading interdenominational religious monthlies in America. Through its wide circulation, it brings inspiring articles and the latest news of religious developments to many families. From the magazine's pages came the initiative for CHRISTIAN HERALD CHILDREN'S HOME and THE BOWERY MISSION, two individually supported not-for-profit corporations.

CHRISTIAN HERALD CHILDREN'S HOME, established in 1894, is the name for a unique and dynamic ministry to disadvantaged children, offering hope and opportunities which would not otherwise be available for reasons of poverty and neglect. The goal is to develop each child's potential and to demonstrate Christian compassion and understanding to children in need.

Mont Lawn is a permanent camp located in Bushkill, Pennsylvania. It is the focal point of a ministry which provides a healthful "vacation with a purpose" to children who without it would be confined to the streets of the city. Up to 1000 children between the ages of 7 and 11 come to Mont Lawn each year.

Christian Herald Children's Home maintains year-round contact with children by means of an *In-City Youth Ministry.* Central to its philosophy is the belief that only through sustained relationships and demonstrated concern can individual lives be truly enriched. Special emphasis is on individual guidance, spiritual and family counseling and tutoring. This follow-up ministry to inner-city children culminates for many in financial assistance toward higher education and career counseling.

THE BOWERY MISSION, located at 227 Bowery, New York City, has since 1879 been reaching out to the lost men on the Bowery, offering them what could be their last chance to rebuild their lives. Every man is fed, clothed and ministered to. Countless numbers have entered the 90-day residential rehabilitation program at the Bowery Mission. A concentrated ministry of counseling, medical care, nutrition therapy, Bible study and Gospel services awakens a man to spiritual renewal within himself.

These ministries are supported solely by the voluntary contributions of individuals and by legacies and bequests. Contributions are tax deductible. Checks should be made out either to CHRISTIAN HERALD CHILDREN'S HOME or to THE BOWERY MISSION.

Administrative Office: 40 Overlook Drive, Chappaqua, New York 10514
Telephone: (914) 769-9000